Mary Burns is a mother of three, a teacher, and has become involved in addiction advocacy since her son's death. She helped spearhead a walk called 'Changing the Face of Addiction,' to help change the stigma of addiction. She has also brought her advocacy to her local state senator and addressed the New Jersey Senate Budget Appropriations Committee about the need for a change to the addiction treatment protocol.

She was honored as an Advocacy Leader in 2017 by the New Jersey chapter of the National Council on Alcoholism and Drug Dependence.

This book is dedicated to my son, Eric, who always wanted to write a book about his struggle.

Mary Burns

SAVING ERIC

A MOTHER'S JOURNEY
THROUGH HER SON'S ADDICTION

AUSTIN MACAULEY PUBLISHERS™

LONDON • CAMBRIDGE • NEW YORK • SHARJAH

Ordering Information:
Quantity sales: special discounts are available on quantity purchases by corporations, associations, and others. For details, contact the publisher at the address below.

Publisher's Cataloging-in-Publication data
Burns, Mary
Saving Eric

ISBN 9781645750987 (Paperback)
ISBN 9781645750994 (Hardback)
ISBN 9781645751007(ePub e-book)

Library of Congress Control Number: 2020904749

www.austinmacauley.com/us

First Published (2020)
Austin Macauley Publishers LLC
40 Wall Street, 28th Floor
New York, NY 10005
USA

mail-usa@austinmacauley.com
+1 (646) 5125767

I want to thank the many people who encouraged me to move forward with this book. This includes my friend, Sandy, who read my first manuscript and insisted that my story should be told. I also want to thank my mother, who read all of my manuscripts many times and encouraged me to have this story published.

I want to thank the Montclair Write Group, who welcomed me and advised me on how to improve my writing. I want to thank my editor, Lorraine Ash, who believed in this project and in me.

Last but not least, I want to thank my children, Jessica and Matthew, for supporting my decision to publish this story.

Table of Content

Author's Note

I focused this narrative on my son's, Eric's, battle with addiction and how he and I fought that struggle together. In consideration of my husband's feelings, I included family members only in certain parts. From the beginning, however, we all lived the story together.

Prologue
June 2009

As soon as Eric signed into the emergency room, the triage nurse took us into her office. Eric leaned forward, gripping his stomach, and answering questions.

In no time, he was in a bed, all one hundred seventy-five pounds of him, doubled over and turning from side to side to get comfortable.

"Before we admit him into detox," a nurse said, "We need to rule out any other possible causes for his pain."

A phlebotomist drew Eric's blood. As he left, a doctor asked questions.

"What do you take?" he asked.

"OxyContin," Eric replied.

"How much?"

"Half a pill."

"How many?"

"Two."

"A day?"

"Yeah," he paused, "Or three."

Sitting quietly, I listened, his every answer, paining me.

OxyContin? An opioid. My nineteen-year-old son is addicted to drugs. How did this happen? He's such a smart kid. What is he thinking?

I wiped my eyes. He partied. He made bad decisions. I knew that. I'd tried talking to him.

"Stop doing drugs," I told him, "Stop partying every night." But I never got far before he argued and, most of the time, spun himself into a rage.

I was concerned but I'd grown up in the seventies and knew many kids who smoked pot. Most turned out just fine. I thought smoking pot was a phase. I thought Eric would get over it.

I looked at my son, lying on the bed, writhing in pain, and clenching his jaw.

As the doctor asked more questions, the whirring in my mind subsided.

"We're not sure your insurance company will approve admitting him into the detox unit," he said.

The nurse must have seen the confusion on my face.

"His drug habit may not be bad enough," she explained.

"What do you mean? How can his drug habit not be bad enough?" I asked, "I thought you were addicted to a substance or not addicted to a substance. How could Eric not be addicted badly enough?"

When the blood work results arrived near midnight, the doctor concluded Eric's pain was due to drug withdrawal.

The next step: calling the insurance company.

Eric was visibly worse. He tossed and turned and moaned.

"We're almost certain the insurance company will not approve his admittance into the detox unit," said a second nurse, "You can wait, if you like or leave. The insurance company should have a final decision in a few hours."

Eric clutched his stomach, his eyes glowing in anger.

"What?" he yelled.

"We'll leave the decision up to you," the nurse told him.

He looked at me.

"Mom, what should I do?"

"I don't know, Eric. I was expecting you would be admitted. I don't know what to tell you."

I didn't want to waste a few hours, if the hospital wasn't going to admit him, but what would we do, if we left?

"It's up to you, Eric," I said.

"Let's get out of here," he said.

He'd taken a brave step. He'd admitted he had a problem. He asked for help, but the hospital, equipped to detox people, wouldn't admit him.

I helped him off the bed. We walked out, Eric walking slowly. As we passed the security station, he spit at the window. A gob of phlegm slid down the glass.

"Eric, no! Stop it!" I yelled, "What are you doing?"

The next day I stayed home from work, thinking I could, somehow, help my son detox. I had absolutely no idea about drug withdrawal or how painful and potentially dangerous it could be.

The two of us stayed in the family room. He lay on the couch, tossing and turning. I sat on the chair next to the couch, watching him, and holding his hand from time to time.

I didn't know where to go or what to do. I opened the phone book and looked under 'Drug Abuse & Addiction Information & Treatment.'

Over the years, my son had faced so many challenges. I'd helped him through a lot. That morning, for the first time, we were locked in a battle larger than both of us. I prayed that my love would be able to save him.

1. Just Amazing
1990–1997

I first laid eyes on my beautiful boy at JFK Airport at 9 a.m. January 9, 1990.

A snowstorm had delayed Korean Air Flight 206. My husband and I waited three hours for its arrival with our daughter, Jessica, who'd also been born in South Korea. She found a balloon in the airport that read 'Welcome' and held it patiently.

We'd been told that Eric weighed only five pounds at birth. So, when the guardians wheeled in two baby boys in gray strollers, I went straight to the smaller one. But I was wrong. He was the bigger one wearing a light blue fleece outfit with white lambs.

The guardians told us the babies had been changed. I tried to feed Eric, so he wouldn't cry on the way home, but he didn't take a bottle.

We buckled him into the back seat of our car next to Jessica. Excited, I sat in front and could hardly wait until we stopped at my mother-in-law's house on the way home, just to show him off. Since she lives with my sister-in-law, Eric also met his three cousins, who came downstairs to see him.

While I changed his diaper, all of them bent over him, talking and trying to get him to smile. My mother-in-law and sister-in-law held him. He didn't fuss.

Just like that, Eric was part of our family.

As he grew, his brilliance impressed us. We only had to tell him something once, maybe twice, and he remembered it.

As a toddler, he sat in front of the television, rocking to videos with songs such as 'Old MacDonald Had a Farm.'

We also admired his imagination, during his preschool years. He loved his pretend kitchen. He gathered all his VELCRO® food and set up elaborate dinners and lunch spreads on the cement hearth by the fireplace. Once he was done cooking, he and I pretended to eat and, of course, everything he made was always delicious.

We played games like Memory. He beat me almost every time.

The two of us also pretended to be Power Rangers. I w₂
was Tommy. All day long, he'd say, "Oh, Mom, Rita Repulsa
have to fight her off."

I'd be, right there, fighting alongside Eric.

In nursery school, my amazing boy made many good friends,
at our house. Often their parents invited Eric to their houses. We   ousy.
Eric seemed happy, excelled at every activity he tried, and took naturally to
sports. He started karate lessons at five years old and earned his black belt in
Tang Soo Do at eight-and-a-half. He played soccer, basketball, and baseball
and was always a starter.

Playing baseball in spring and summer, he was almost always an all-star.
When his coaches started a fall ball team, he played eight months of the year.
By middle school, he made the Babe Ruth team.

For two summers, he played on the county all-star team. Twice, he played
at the local minor league stadium as an all-star. We traveled all over northern
and central New Jersey to cheer Eric on.

In elementary school, Eric earned straight As, learning easily and doing
homework quickly and willingly. Halfway through third grade, he came home
crying of boredom because he finished his in-class assignments so quickly; he
had a lot of downtime.

His fourth-grade teacher occupied him during those downtimes, making
Eric her Internet 'expert.' When his assignments were done, he looked up
information for her on the worldwide web; then, a new phenomenon. She
motivated him and made him feel important. I was grateful.

During a parent-teacher conference, she asked an unusual question.

"Is there anything going on at home?"

"Why do you ask? Is Eric having problems in school?"

She shrugged her shoulders.

"I just get a feeling something is wrong," she said.

I meet her gaze, wondering why she thought that. Eric had never gotten in
trouble at school and I'd never received a phone call about his behavior from
any of his teachers or the principal.

"I was diagnosed with skin cancer last year," I said. "It's possible Eric is
upset about that."

I assured her I'd speak to him.

I left the conference shocked but amazed at how perceptive she was. Eric
had begun to show troubling behavior at home. I felt it was a private matter,
though, and wasn't sure what to tell her. But she was correct; something was
very wrong.

2. Screaming
1997

The first time I realized something wasn't right was a night like any other. I heated up the tomato sauce I'd made earlier that day, as I cooked pasta for dinner. My two sons, Eric and Matthew, put away their art supplies when their sister returned home from her dance lesson.

"Can I hang my new picture on the refrigerator?" Matthew asked.

"Of course," I replied.

Using a magnet, he proudly hung his latest masterpiece amid others.

Eric ran upstairs to put his picture in his room. Sometimes, he tacked his pictures on the bulletin board on the desk in his room or placed them in one of his desk drawers. He liked to save his drawings, which was fun. Sometimes, we took them out to see how they'd changed over the years.

My kitchen smelled delicious. Thursday was pasta night in my family, since my childhood. As a kid, I walked home from school anticipating the aroma and delicious meal that awaited me that evening. I still looked forward to Thursdays as that night's menu featured my family's favorite; spaghetti and meatballs.

"Dinner is ready," I told Jessica and Matthew, "Wash your hands."

They took turns using the sink in the bathroom off of the kitchen.

I walked to the bottom of the stairs.

"Eric, dinner is ready. Wash your hands and come downstairs!"

As I turned back toward the kitchen, I heard, "Aaaah! Aaaah! Aaaah!"

Eric was screaming.

My heart skipped a beat. I raced up the stairs, thinking he was hurt. When I reached his room, he stood in the middle, screaming at the top of his lungs.

"Aaaah! Aaaah! Aaaah!"

He didn't appear hurt. When I moved closer, he extended his hands in front of him, palms toward me, and backed away. He didn't seem to focus on anything in particular. He stared straight ahead with a detached, vacant look in his eyes.

Scared, I wondered if he even knew who I was.

Again, I approached.

Again, he put out his hands and backed away.

"Aaaah! Aaaah!"

My heart pounded. I didn't understand. A few minutes earlier, he quietly played downstairs with his brother. *What could have happened in that small amount of time?*

"Aaaah!"

"Eric, what's happening?" I yelled, "Eric!"

He didn't seem to hear me. He continued to stare and scream and not let me anywhere near him. I quickly looked around the room. *Is anything out of the ordinary?* The room was neat. The beds were made and the windows, closed. No toys were on the floor.

"What's the matter? What's the matter?" I asked.

He didn't answer. He just stared and screamed. A sick feeling came over me. I didn't know what to do. The screaming went on and on.

Then, as suddenly as it started, it stopped. He cried and let me hug him. I held him close and rubbed his back.

"What's the matter?" I asked, "What happened? Are you hurt? Why were you screaming like that?"

He didn't answer. He just sobbed and let me hold him.

Finally, the sobbing subsided. He was calm. I loosened my hold.

"Why were you screaming? What happened?"

He returned my gaze but didn't answer.

I pulled him close to me as we walked down the hallway with my hand on his shoulder. We stopped at the top of the staircase. Jessica and Matthew stared at us from the foot of the stairs. They looked confused.

"Did Eric get hurt?" Jessica asked.

"No, he was just upset about something," I said.

I looked at Eric and kissed him. We walked down the stairs and into the kitchen.

"What happened?" Jessica asked Eric, "Why were you crying?"

"What's wrong?" Matthew added.

Eric shrugged his shoulders.

They all sat at the table as I brought over the food. While we ate, I turned to Jessica and Eric.

"Did anything different happen today in school?" I asked, "Did anything exciting happen in school?"

"We didn't do anything today," Jessica said.

"We are doing a project in language arts," Eric said.

I perked up, happy to hear him talk.

"What's the project about?"

"We needed to make a book cover for the story that we just read."

Still trying to figure out what made him scream, I pressed the issue.

"Who did you work with on the project?"

"I worked with Joey, Kyle, and Tom."

"Did you agree on what to do or did you argue about how to do the project?"

"No, we didn't fight and we made a cool cover we all liked."

"What did you do on the playground?" I continued.

"We played tag on the playground like we always do," he said, "I was 'it' but not for long because I'm a fast runner."

He smiled.

"I believe that because you are a fast runner! Who did you play tag with?"

He shrugged his shoulders.

"Just my friends that I always play with."

I kept asking questions, hoping Eric would say something that clued me in on why he screamed.

Later that night, I looked through his backpack in case I'd missed something during my usual afternoon check for returned papers and homework. I found a few graded papers; all with one-hundreds on them. Typical. He also had math homework and, as usual, he'd done it that afternoon, without complaint on his own.

I looked over his homework to see if he'd done the problems correctly. As expected, they all looked right.

At eight o'clock, the kids relaxed and watched television in the family room.

"It's time to get ready for bed," I told them, "Turn off the TV."

They obeyed and went upstairs. Once they were in pajamas, I went into Eric and Matthew's room and read to them; a bedtime ritual since they were babies.

I took turns reading with Eric, since he was in second grade and a very good reader. He read the left page and I, the right page.

While reading, I was very animated. Eric tried to imitate me. We laughed at how silly we sounded. After reading, I tucked in each of them, kissed them good night, and turned off the bedroom light.

I sat next to Jessica on her bed and let her read to me from the Baby-Sitters' Club series. After ten minutes, I kissed her good night.

"Good night, sweetie," I said, turning off the light.

At a quarter to nine, my husband came home from work. I prepared a dish for him.

"Before dinner, Eric was in his room and screamed," I said, "and I mean screamed! He just stood in the middle of his room and screamed at the top of his lungs. It was weird. He wouldn't let me near him. It was like he didn't know who I was or that I was even in the room."

"Maybe something happened in school," my husband replied, not overly concerned.

"That's what I thought but if something happened, he didn't say anything. When he came home, he acted normal and seemed happy. I don't understand it."

"Hopefully, it won't happen again."

I still thought something in school must have bothered him but I couldn't be sure. I left the kitchen, still confused and shaken by the incident but hopeful the screaming was a one-time event. I sat on my favorite chair in the family room, put the television on, and relaxed for an hour before going to bed.

3. Adoption Talk
1998–1999

The screaming tantrums continued sporadically, once every four or five months. Every time, they frightened me and left me at a loss.

After each incident, I talked with Eric and felt he was better afterwards. I always thought it wouldn't happen again. It always did.

Finally, I realized Eric had never inquired about his adoption. *Perhaps this causes his tantrums?*

His sister was only four when she suddenly said, "Mommy, tell me about my other mommy."

Eric had always known he was adopted but never asked for particulars. I had never volunteered the information.

One day in his room, I seized my opportunity.

"Do you want to learn more about your birth mother?" I asked.

He burst into tears and nodded. I hugged him and waited for him to calm down.

"Do you want me to tell you what I know about your birth mother and father?"

He nodded.

"Yes," he said.

I left his room and returned with the envelope that contained his birth information. I told him his birth mother's name and read the rest.

"She was twenty-one, when she gave birth to you," I said, "She graduated high school and worked in a factory. She is the third child in a family of two boys and four girls."

I stopped and interjected.

"This means that if you lived in South Korea with her, you would have two uncles and three aunts."

I returned to the sheet.

"She is described as introversive, which means she is quiet. She is 160 centimeters tall and weighs 55 kilograms. If you want to, we can figure out how many pounds and feet that is later."

I continued.

"After finishing high school, she moved to Incheon City and worked at the factory while living with her elder sister. She gave birth to this baby, that's you, at DaeIn Hospital in Buk-gu, Incheon City on July 31, 1989. After delivery, it says, she was not allowed to bring up the baby by herself and avoided telling about the bio-father. She thought it best that she let the baby be adopted to a good home that could provide sufficient support and much love. After careful consideration, the bio-mother referred her baby to our Incheon branch for adoption on August 1, 1989, asking that her baby be adopted to a good home."

Under the section marked 'Status,' two boxes are checked: 'illegitimate' and 'abandoned by mother.'

No information was available about Eric's birth father as the sheet just stated they were an unmarried couple. I kept reading.

"It says your mother carried you to full term, Eric, and that you were delivered by Caesarean section because of breech presentation. You were 2.9 kilograms, at birth."

I explained what all that meant. Eric listened quietly.

I read it to him again to give him time to comprehend.

"Do you have any questions?" I asked.

He didn't. He seemed okay with what he'd learned.

I continued to read the information his South Korean foster mother provided about the five-and-a-half months she had cared for him. The sheet stated how often he was fed, how much formula he drank, how well he slept, and when he was fussy. It also described his bathroom habits, how often she changed his diaper, and how he enjoyed his bath.

"She says you easily stopped crying when you were held," I read.

The foster mother provided notes about Eric's motor development, too, writing that he was 'startled by a sudden bell,' 'follows the red yarn with eyes,' and is 'generally hot-tempered.'

Again, I read it all a second time.

"Do you have any questions, Eric?" I asked.

"No," he said.

We went downstairs where he played with Jessica and Matthew. He didn't cry. He didn't seem upset or bothered by what I'd read.

Happy, I stood in the doorway of the family room and watched him fall back into his routine. I couldn't believe he'd bottled up all that emotion. Why hadn't he just asked me about his adoption like his sister did?

Even though Eric seemed fine, I wanted him to see a therapist. My husband was against therapy, though. I abided by his wishes and hoped Eric wouldn't have any more screaming tantrums.

After five uneventful months, it happened again. The outburst was more extreme. Its intensity frightened me, Jessica, and Matthew. When Eric erupted in the past, his brother and sister had been downstairs, where they didn't hear the intensity of the screaming.

This time, they watched television in my bedroom when the tantrum started. As I ran toward Eric's screams, I saw them on my bed, crying and hugging each other.

When I entered Eric's room, I was shocked. He shook his big and heavy four-drawer dresser.

"I want to die!" he screamed, "I hope this falls on top of me! I want to die!"

I immediately got between him and the dresser.

"Stop. Stop!" I yelled.

Still intent on knocking over the dresser, he pushed me out of the way. I pushed back, not allowing him near the dresser. He fought back, trying to reach the dresser.

"I want to die! I want this to fall on top of me! I want to die!"

My body shook. My stomach twisted in knots. I couldn't believe what was happening. I couldn't get him to stop. The episode seemed to go on and on.

I continued to push him away from the dresser but he fought back while staring blankly and screaming, "I want to die! I want to die!"

He didn't seem to recognize me. Neither did he seem to fully comprehend how the dresser could hurt him.

"If you don't stop," I yelled, "I will call the police!"

Finally, he emerged from his trancelike state.

I knelt to hug him.

"Eric, what's wrong? Why were you trying to hurt yourself? I love you and I don't want anything to happen to you. Can you tell me why you were trying to hurt yourself?"

I held him tightly until he finished sobbing.

Once he was calm, I went into my room to comfort Jessica and Matthew, who were still on my bed, crying. I hugged them and soothed their fears as much as I could but I couldn't explain what had just happened because I didn't understand it myself.

Once all my children were calm, we continued with our day. We ate dinner, did homework, and played a game. Eric was his usual happy self, as if nothing had happened. I was grateful but confused.

When my husband came home, I was still shaken and upset.

"I'm going to bring Eric to therapy," I announced, "He had another outburst and this time he tried to hurt himself and he scared Jessica and Matthew."

He agreed.

My quest to find a therapist began with my health insurance company handbook. Much to my surprise, everyone listed didn't see children. I called the county mental health services line and asked for a referral. A week later I was given the name of a therapist, who dealt with children and adoption issues.

Eric and I went to see the therapist once a week. Eric seemed comfortable with her but never shared what they talked about. After each session, we went out for dinner. He talked about school, sports, and playing with his friends. Animated, he laughed, smiled, and joked around, like he always did.

After four months of therapy, I approached the therapist.

"Do you think his adoption bothers him?" I asked.

"Yes, his adoption may be bothersome for him," she said.

"Can you explain to me what he has said about it or why it bothers him?"

"I can't share that with you," she said.

"Why not?"

"To protect his privacy."

I was taken aback. Eric was ten years old. Wasn't he too young for privacy to be an issue? And how was I supposed to help him if I didn't know what bothered him?

I wasn't convinced four months of therapy had helped Eric but the tantrums had stopped.

4. Scary Thoughts
1999–2003

A few quiet months followed. Then, one night, for no apparent reason, Eric had another tantrum.

"I'm going to commit suicide. I want to kill myself. I want to die!" he screamed.

I couldn't believe a ten-year-old knew what suicide was and couldn't imagine where he had learned about it.

The next day, I was at my pediatrician's office with Matthew and asked the doctor for a private conference. I explained the situation.

He riffled through his desk and wrote on a piece of paper.

"This is the number of a mental health clinic," he said, "You need to make an appointment for Eric to see a therapist. It's not good he has this type of thoughts."

I called the next day but the clinic couldn't see Eric. They didn't see people who lived in our county. Once again, I was left looking for help.

A few days later, I sat with Eric.

"Why were you screaming the other day?" I asked. "Why did you say you wanted to kill yourself? Where did you learn about suicide?"

"I don't know," he replied, shrugging his shoulders.

Needing him to understand his outbursts were not acceptable, I took a different tack.

After the next one, I grounded him during the next baseball practice. He was upset but he controlled himself for a few weeks.

Finally, his father witnessed a tantrum and forbade Eric from attending his next baseball practice. The coach was upset but supportive. I don't believe the coach understood why we took such a stance. To him, Eric was a pleasure to coach, an athlete who always put his best forward.

At school, Eric still excelled. He was even put in the gifted and talented program. Nothing was difficult for him. Elementary and middle school were easy. He breezed through each grade, until eighth grade.

Eric matured early. In the summer between seventh and eighth grades, he had a tremendous growth spurt and stood about 5 feet 5 inches; much taller than most of his friends. For the first time, he struggled in school, especially in algebra. Like most math subjects, algebra requires practice. Eric was not willing to put in the time. I offered help; he declined it.

At that point, Eric grew argumentative. His tantrums became more regular. He said things that concerned me, even when he wasn't having an episode.

One evening, I walked into his room to kiss him good night. He lay on his bed in the dark.

"What's the matter? Are you feeling okay?" I asked.

He stared at the ceiling.

"Mom, I'm really a bad person," he said, "You don't know what goes on in my mind. I'm *really* a bad person."

I felt nauseous and weak. I walked closer to him.

"What do you mean? Why do you think you're a bad person?"

He shook his head.

"Mom, you don't know what goes on in my mind. I really *am* a bad person."

I walked to his bed, sat next to him, and made eye contact.

"You are *not* a bad person, Eric. You were raised to know the difference between right and wrong and you have power over your thoughts. When you have these thoughts, you should say a prayer and ask God for help."

He turned his head and looked at me.

"I do pray but these bad thoughts still come into my head."

I held his hand and closed my eyes.

"Dear Lord, please protect Eric and help him understand that he is a good person. Please guide him and help him make good decisions."

I hugged and kissed him good night.

As I left the room, the sick feeling in my stomach worsened. *What's happening to the amazing boy I raised? Why is he having such troubling thoughts?*

The rages, on their own, were difficult enough to deal with. Hearing him call himself bad truly frightened me.

After that, I said a simple prayer with Eric each night, before he went to sleep. He sat next to me on his bed and listened quietly. Often, he added a short prayer of his own.

I believed that Eric's thoughts truly scared him. I prayed, he prayed. He even took my picture of Jesus for his room. I didn't ask him why but I was certain it made him feel safe.

5. Torment
Summer 2003

Up until the summer between eighth grade and freshman year in high school, I hadn't told anyone about Eric's tantrums. Then, I had to. His outbursts left me physically, mentally, and emotionally drained and I wasn't sure I could handle them much longer.

He needed help! I needed help!

In desperation, I drove to my pediatrician's office and asked, through tears, to see him right away, even though I didn't have an appointment. I didn't know who else to tell. He was a doctor and he had adopted kids, too. I poured out my story.

"The tantrums used to happen every four to six months but now it's much more often," I explained, "Anything I do works for a little while but, then, the tantrums return. And they're getting more scary, as he gets bigger. He may suffer from mental illness. I just don't know what to do anymore."

"Will you be bringing him in for a physical before school?" he asked.

"Yes, I have a sport's physical scheduled for next week."

"I'll talk to him about his behavior next week. Maybe, we can get this straightened out."

"That would be great. At this point, I need help."

I left, still upset, but hopeful that the doctor could make a difference.

The next week I sat in the waiting room, while Eric saw the pediatrician. Once the physical was complete, the doctor called me into the exam room.

"I've spoken to Eric about his behavior and I think that he is okay and that he will behave himself from now on," he said, facing me but staring at Eric. "I've told him how inappropriate his behavior is and I don't expect him to behave like that anymore."

I was confused and upset. I knew Eric was not okay and certain his behavior wouldn't stop. How could the doctor make such an assessment in such a short time? I thought he'd send Eric to therapy to figure out what made him rage. I thought he'd tell me Eric has a mental illness, so I could get him help, get me help.

Eric leered at me from the exam table. I could tell he wasn't happy I'd brought him to the pediatrician for a talk. I could tell he was embarrassed that someone outside the family knew.

We left the doctor's office without a resolution to our problem.

A few days later, I walked into Eric's room one afternoon, as he lay on his bed. I handed him a notebook.

"I want you to write in this notebook all the scary thoughts that come into your mind. Write down anything that bothers you," I said, "Maybe, then, you'll feel better and stop having screaming tantrums."

I wasn't finished. I'd thought this through.

"I also want you to write a letter to your birth mother. I think it bothers you that you're adopted. Writing a letter might help you get the anger out. Writing might feel better than screaming."

I'd asked many times if he was upset he was adopted but he just shrugged his shoulders and didn't say anything. I couldn't help but think he was upset by his birth mother giving him up. Did he feel rejected? Unworthy? Thrown away? Not good enough?

Maybe, he thought he'd hurt my feelings if he talked to me about it. I didn't know. I just realized I couldn't handle his anger anymore. I needed it to stop.

After one episode, Eric walked to a friend's house and stayed overnight. When I picked him up the next day, the friend's mother invited me inside.

"How was Eric last night?" I asked her, "Did he seem upset?"

"No. We love having Eric over. He's always a pleasure to have around. Actually, he had us laughing at the dinner table last night. He can be so funny."

I was relieved but perplexed. How could a child so troubled at home be such an angel elsewhere?

Worry set in as puberty approached. I tried everything I could think of. Yet, my amazing child kept slipping away from me. Why is my son tormented by thoughts he can't control? I called his thoughts 'monsters.' Where did they come from? And, why wouldn't they go away?

Could we handle such a troubled child? I shared my fear with my husband, who wasn't as concerned. Fear became my constant companion, though. Not just for myself but for the rest of my family and Eric. When he spun into an uncontrollable rage, he changed into a threatening young man, who couldn't be reasoned with.

The amazing boy I'd loved and raised was becoming someone I didn't recognize.

6. "Safe Spot"
Early 2004

During high school, Eric often told me his life was a struggle.

"It's so hard, Mom," he said, "Sometimes, it's really hard for me to make good decisions."

Struggle! How in the world could his life be a struggle? Why would he even say such a thing?

Eric grew up in a loving family, in a beautiful home, and neighborhood surrounded by woods. He never wanted for anything. Not food to eat or clothes to wear or friends to play with. He excelled at anything he tried.

But he was right; it was a struggle. Not only for Eric for some unknown reason but for our family and me, too. The screaming episodes continued into high school, growing more frequent and scary over time, always leaving me drained and exhausted.

I still talked to him about his adoption and the rages but he always insisted they had nothing to do with each other.

"You and dad are the only parents I've ever known, so how can I be mad at my birth mother?" he said, "I was so young when I was adopted. I don't remember anything, so how can something I don't remember bother me?"

But I was convinced of the connection. After many phone calls, I found an available male therapist on my insurance plan, who saw teenagers. I thought Eric might have more respect for a male figure because his rages were directed at me. He rarely raged at his father.

I was excited with the discovery but the thrill was short-lived.

The second I met the therapist, I knew the relationship wouldn't work. He wore a nice pair of slacks, a sport coat, and a bow tie and greeted us warmly, shaking both our hands when he introduced himself. But I knew Eric wouldn't relate to his formality, which disappointed me. By then, I realized how few male therapists work with teenagers.

Even so, Eric met with him weekly for about two months. During these sessions, we sometimes met with the therapist together. Other times, we went in separately. When I was in the room with Eric and the therapist, Eric never said very much. He came across as a typical teenager.

Driving Eric back and forth to our therapy sessions became a battle. He hated going. The second I pulled out of our driveway, a rage began.

"Why do I have to go to therapy?" he screamed, "There isn't anything wrong with me. It's your fuckin' problem that you can't handle me! He's a fuckin' idiot. He's not going to be able to help me. Therapy is so stupid. Therapists don't do anything to help you. You just sit and talk to a person you don't know and they don't tell you anything! I don't want to talk about my life to a stranger! I don't want to go and I shouldn't have to go! Why the fuck do I have to go?"

He went on the entire twenty minutes. His cursing made driving difficult. I tried to stay calm but he was unbearable. It was a wonder I didn't have an accident.

By the time we arrived at the therapist's office, I was near tears. I needed the therapy, if only Eric wasn't with me.

Soon, I dreaded therapy night but I was determined to help him. We had to get to the bottom of his terrible outbursts. I wanted the son I knew and raised. I wanted my child back!

Though the sessions were short-lived, I learned two important things.

First, the therapist told me the behavior of an adopted child can sometimes be extreme. He'd developed a theory: an adopted child often tests their adoptive parents to the point of almost breaking them; just to be sure the parents really love them and won't give them back.

He made sense and was, somewhat, reassuring, though by that point, I would have hoped Eric knew we wouldn't give him back. Also, the theory didn't help Eric or me control his angry outbursts.

Second, the therapist concluded that Eric may very well be angry with his birth mother for not keeping him.

"You, his adoptive mother, are the closest thing he has to his birth mother," he said, "So, Eric directs the anger he feels toward her at you."

Essentially, I had taken her place. This was good and bad news.

Good, because Eric obviously felt comfortable enough with me to let his true feelings show. He trusted me.

Bad, because his behavior was so extreme, it wasn't healthy for me physically, emotionally, or mentally. I had become Eric's proverbial, not literal – punching bag. I didn't want the job. I'd never formally accepted it. Nonetheless, that's what I had become.

Put another way, the therapist told me I was Eric's 'safe spot,' the one he knew would listen to him, the one to whom he felt comfortable releasing his anger, and the one he knew would always love him. As a parent, I suppose I should have been honored but I was not. I was drained and horrified at the prospect of the many years to come.

I didn't seek out a new therapist, immediately. Even with Eric volatile as he was, we still had periods of normalcy. Sometimes, he was the most loving, cooperative child. He always told me he loved me and when he crossed the line, always apologized.

Sometimes, I still saw the amazing Eric of his early years. I became convinced there were two of him: good Eric and angry Eric.

Good Eric was the child I knew I raised, still able to raise his head above the insanity seeping into his mind.

Angry Eric was the child I didn't recognize and knew I didn't raise. I didn't understand why the love and encouragement we'd shown him couldn't override his possible feelings of neglect and anger against his birth mother.

I appreciated his loving gestures between rages but they didn't make up for the abuse I, sometimes, endured.

And the rages always returned, even evolving to have a new component. When Eric was in an altered state of mind, usually after school, he threatened to kill himself with my large carving knife.

While screaming, he grabbed the knife from the block next to the stove, put it to his neck, and yelled, "I'm going to slit my throat! It'll be your fault, if I slit my throat! I don't want to be a part of this stupid family anymore! I can't stand living here anymore!"

"Put down that knife!" I screamed back, "Stop! Don't! Stop! Put down that knife!"

Somehow, I kept my wits about me and talked him into putting down the knife.

Once he calmed down, I talked to him about what had just happened.

"Mom, I would never hurt anyone or myself," he said, almost laughing, "I wasn't really going to slit my throat!"

I couldn't be so sure. When he was in a rage, I believed his thinking was so skewed that he was capable of anything.

At times, I threatened to call 911 and have him committed to a mental hospital.

"Do that and you'll be sorry," he said.

I was never exactly sure what 'being sorry' meant but, fearing for myself and other family members, who he routinely threatened, I never called. He regularly lost his sense of reality. He loved us but would that be enough to stop him from carrying out his threats?

Between these bouts of insanity, Eric and I did things together. He suggested we go out to lunch or asked me to see the high school play, when one of his friends was in it.

He kept his room impeccable, helped me put away groceries, and cleaned up the kitchen at night, without being asked.

Then, suddenly, without warning, all hell broke loose.

I felt as if I was walking a tightrope; trying to keep Eric's behavior in check and myself and the rest of the family safe. Driving home from work, I sometimes cried because I didn't know what I'd find when I got there; the calm Eric or the one who raged at the smallest provocation.

Some days, I didn't even want to go home. I wanted to run away. Teaching full-time, running the kids to their activities, attending their games, making sure they did their homework, making dinner, and doing all the other daily chores was exhausting in itself. Add a raging teenager to the mix and life became unbearable.

At times, I didn't think I could hold myself together. I wasn't sure I could go on but I did, determined to save my son from the insanity hijacking his brain.

After a break from therapy, with the rages still extremely volatile, I researched types of mental illness; convincing myself Eric suffered with either borderline personality disorder or bipolar disorder. Neither the last therapist or the pediatrician thought he was mentally ill but I think that's because he presented himself as an ordinary teenager, when he wasn't at home.

I asked a caseworker at my school for a referral. I went to the first appointment alone to check out the therapist and tell him about the rages and my concerns about mental illness. I liked his more casual demeanor, thinking it would help Eric open up.

He agreed to meet Eric. I made an appointment for the following week.

Eric went without much complaining, leading me to believe he felt more comfortable with this therapist. They were alone for most of the forty-five-minute sessions. I went in for a small portion toward the end.

7. Escalation
Fall 2004–Spring 2005

One of my biggest concerns besides the rages was the profane language that came out of Eric's mouth.

He used the f-word all the time. He didn't care that he said it or that it bothered me. My other kids didn't curse and I didn't understand why he had to.

He said anything; even calling me things no kid should ever call their mother.

"What do you think you're cool? What are you talking like this for?" I said, "What is your problem? What do you think you're tough?"

"Don't be so stupid," he said, "I'm not trying to be cool and I don't have a problem. This is just who I am!"

"It shouldn't be who you are. Your father and I don't swear, so why do you have to? I don't know why you think swearing is okay. It's not!"

Once, he told me that two of his friends treated their mother poorly.

"Do they talk to their mothers like that?" I once asked him.

"Mom, you should hear how they talk to their mothers. Worse."

He could have done the right thing and told his buddies, "You don't talk to your mother like that."

He could have walked away. Instead, he did it himself. Eric was always drawn to the negative.

Sick of hearing his mouth, one day, when his friends sat around our kitchen table, I let out a string of curse words at every opportunity. I wanted Eric to hear what he sounded like. I wanted him to embarrass him.

He left the table, came over to me, and put his arm around my shoulder.

"Mom," he said gently, "Why are you talking that way?"

If I made an impression, it didn't last long. He continued with his disgusting mouth.

After a couple of months, Eric tired of therapy again, and the car rages resumed. I was tired of the nonsense and frustrated that, no matter what I did, he had these angry outbursts. *How am I supposed to keep loving him and yet take so much abuse from him?*

One day, I rushed home from work to take Eric to therapy only to find him standing in the kitchen. He looked straight at me.

"I'm not going."

He refused flat out to get into the car. I didn't know what to do.

"You need to go so we can find out why you always have these screaming fits," I said, struggling to stay calm, "Therapy should be able to help you feel better about things and…"

"I'm not going! I don't want to go. I already told you therapy is stupid," he yelled, "All you do is talk to a stranger about things and they don't tell you anything! Why do I fuckin' have to go? I'm not fuckin' going!"

"Get in the car!" I fired back, "You have to keep your appointment!"

But he stood his ground.

I saw the therapist by myself. When I walked into his office, I was in tears.

"Eric refused to come," I said.

"So why are *you* here?" he asked.

I sat on the couch, still crying.

"I don't know what to do anymore. I don't know how to stop his outbursts. He won't come to therapy and even though, he seems better after we talk after a rage, they always return. What am I supposed to do? I can't stand this anymore. I did some research and I think he might suffer from mental illness," I went on, "I realize the last therapist and my pediatrician don't think so, but he must! What else could cause such angry outbursts? I think he either suffers from borderline personality disorder or bipolar disorder."

"It's possible he suffers from mental illness," he replied, "You would have to take him to a psychiatrist for that type of diagnosis. I'll give you the name of one you can bring him to, if that's what you want."

I took the psychiatrist's card from him, still not convinced he thought Eric was mentally ill. Now *I* had to somehow force this uncooperative, cursing, and verbally abusive child to yet another appointment.

Although, I tried to keep Eric's behavior confidential, some people found out. A couple of neighbors heard yelling or saw me upset. I opened up to them. I didn't want to but I'd bottled up so much emotion that, as soon as they asked how I was, I cried.

They listened without being judgmental of Eric or me, which was very helpful.

For others, who suspected I had issues with Eric, I had a ready reply.

"He's my tough one," I said, never going into detail, though that was difficult to sustain with each passing rage. Talking to others made me feel better. I needed to worry about myself.

I looked into self-help groups for parents with children who suffer from mental illness but I never went to one.

By then, my husband realized Eric wasn't well. Since he often was at work when the rages occurred, he didn't experience the level of anger his son displayed.

One day, after I told him about a rage, he asked, "What did you say to get him so angry?"

How dare he!

"Why would you think it was something I said?" I replied with anger impossible to suppress.

He never admonished his son. He never once said, "Don't ever let me hear that you talk to your mother like that again."

He didn't understand that normal conversation between a teenager and a parent set off Eric. I asked Eric about school-grades, homework, projects that were due, and what he did with his friends. The topics were normal. His responses were not.

Toward the end of sophomore year, the outbursts escalated. Eric was so out of control one afternoon that I could not calm him down. His screaming, threats, and behavior were so severe that I feared for myself and my son, Matthew.

So, I did it, I called 911.

While we waited for the police, Eric was truly in an altered state of mind. He ran in and out of the house, screaming, "Oh my God, the police are coming. Oh my God, I can't believe that you called the police!"

A tearful Matthew begged me, "Mom, call 911 back and tell them the police don't have to come."

"You know I can't do that. The police come once you call 911, even if you call them back and tell them everything is okay."

I waited outside for the police. I would not go back inside as long as Eric was there. I would not give him an opportunity to hurt me. Outside, with neighbors around me, I felt safer; though, not completely safe. I stood by the curb, helplessly watching Eric run in and out of the house, screaming, with no control over his mind and actions.

A neighbor hugged me and I burst into tears. I'd never cried that hard in my life.

After two officers arrived, Eric instantly calmed down. They sat him at the kitchen table and interrogated him.

"What happened to make you so angry that your mother had to call 911?"

He shrugged his shoulders.

"I don't know," he mumbled.

They asked again, "Why did you get so angry at your mother?"

Again, he mumbled, "I don't know. She was asking me about schoolwork and my grades."

I stood behind him, across from the officers, shaking my head.

The police looked at him.

"Your mother was asking about school? That's what made you start screaming? Questions like that shouldn't make you scream, so that your mother has to have us come to your house."

Eric didn't respond.

The officers stayed for ten minutes, staring at him as he sat at the kitchen table. Before they left, one of them sternly told Eric, "If your mother calls 911 again and we have to come back here, we'll take you into custody. Don't make it so your mother has to call us again!"

Eric listened quietly. I was glad for the threat.

They looked at me.

"If he should start screaming again, call us," the other officer said, "We'll come back and bring him to the station."

I was hoping I wouldn't have to, but I was certainly ready to.

After they left, Eric stood up.

"Mom," he asked, "do you want a cup of tea?"

He made tea for me, Matthew, and himself and we all sat and enjoyed a calm conversation. The rest of the day passed pleasantly and without incident.

That day, as in the past, Eric seemed sorry for putting me through such torment. When he was in a rage, I was convinced he wasn't in control of his emotions and actions. *When will this end? Not just for me but for my son; the amazing child I raised, the child with so much promise I'd grown to love.*

8. Silent Strength
Summer 2005

Late, one peaceful summer evening between sophomore and junior year, Eric, Matthew, and I were home alone in the family room. My husband was traveling on business and Jessica was away at school.

"Mom, can you bring me to Don's house?" Eric asked.

"I really can't. I'm just too tired," I said. "Have your friend come here, if you want to hang out with him. He can stay overnight, if you want him to."

With that, Eric stood up from the couch and paced, his agitation visibly growing.

"Do you want to watch a movie?" I asked.

He did not answer.

The tension rose.

"Is there a certain show you want to watch? We can change the channel. Do you want to play a game?"

He paced, ignoring my questions.

I'm too exhausted for a rage. Please, Lord, let him calm down. I don't have the strength tonight.

"I'm sick of living in this fuckin' house! I can't stand being here! Why can't I go out tonight?" Eric screamed, "Why are you so tired that you can't bring me to my friend's house? I don't want to stay in the fuckin' house with you! I hate you and everything about this family! I don't want to have my friends here! I don't want to watch a movie or a TV show with you! I don't want to do anything with you! I don't want to live here anymore! I hate living in this stupid house!"

I tried to keep a calm demeanor but I was too tired. Tears rolled down my face. My crying fueled his anger. He lashed out at me verbally but also screamed at his brother.

"How can you stand to live here?" he yelled at Matthew, "What's fuckin' wrong with you?"

Matthew was a tough kid, who'd long ago accepted the facts of life with Eric. This time, though, he also cried. He seemed frightened by the intensity of Eric's anger unleased, for the first time, directly at him.

Matthew's crying struck a sensitive chord in Eric.

"Sorry, Matt, I didn't mean to get you upset. I'm not angry with you, just her," He pointed at me, "I love you, brother. It's just her. I can't stand her! It's only her I want to hurt. I would never hurt you."

The rage, though it seemed to last an eternity, probably was over in ten minutes. Somehow, through my exhaustion, I got Eric to go to his room. He calmed down near midnight. I wouldn't allow myself to fall sleep until I knew Eric was asleep. Only then would I feel safe.

So, I stayed in the family room, mindlessly watching television with the cell phone in my hand, in case he returned and raged again.

The next morning I called the psychiatrist recommended by the last therapist. I called early because I decided that Eric needed to be seen that very day. At that point, I didn't care if they diagnosed him as bipolar, depressed, or nothing at all. He needed medication to stop these uncontrolled outbursts.

The psychiatrist's staff was not in. I left a desperate message, "My son needs to be seen immediately. He had a rage last night and threatened to kill himself and everyone in the family."

They called back.

"He sounds suicidal," they told me, "Take him to the emergency room immediately."

My nephew was staying over and I didn't feel comfortable leaving him and Matthew alone. I called my mother.

"Can you come up?" I said. "I have to take Eric to the hospital."

She walked in the door at ten o'clock in the morning. I, immediately, handed her a cordless phone.

"I'm going up to get Eric. If you hear screaming, call 911."

Grabbing the other cordless phone, I went to Eric's room and woke him up as gently as I could.

"What?" he asked.

He wasn't happy but he was certainly calmer than the night before.

"I called the doctor and he told me to take you to the hospital," I said, "You have five minutes to get dressed and get in the car. If you don't, I'll call 911 and have you brought to the hospital in a straitjacket."

Surprisingly, he complied. Within a couple of minutes, he was in the car. The ride to the hospital was quiet. He slept most of the way.

Still shaken from the previous night's episode, I burst into tears when telling the security guard at the front desk why we were there. Seeing me, an ER nurse quickly took Eric into the back. The security guard came around from behind the desk and put his arm on my shoulders.

"He's in good hands," he said, "There are good people here and they will be able to help you."

A few minutes later, I composed myself and joined Eric in the ER.

For once, he showed his true colors to someone outside the family. He acted like the 'badass boy' he had become in front of the doctors and nurses, who examined him. Someone from the mental health department was called.

I hoped they'd admit Eric and keep him for a few days. The last thing I wanted was to take an angry, suicidal kid home with me. My hope was short-lived.

After four hours in the ER, the mental health worker approached me.

"We cannot admit him but we do feel he needs psychiatric help," he said, "Right now, all our psychiatrists are busy, so you'll need to bring him back in the morning for an evaluation. I've made an appointment for you to come back tomorrow at eight o'clock."

I was shocked. I was upset. I could not believe they were sending a nasty, suicidal kid home with me. I broke down again.

To my amazement, right in front of my son, the mental health worker approached me.

"What's the matter?" he asked.

How do I explain to him just how horrible Eric's anger is? How do I tell him I don't feel safe bringing him home? How do I say how difficult it will be to bring him back the next day! Inside, I screamed, *take me into another room so we can talk in private!*

But I could not comfortably reply in front of Eric.

We left the hospital after I calmed down. Thankfully, Eric was quiet during the ride home. When we arrived home, we were both hungry.

"Mom, do you want a cup of tea?" Good Eric asked. "Are you hungry? I can fix us lunch."

He could not dote over me enough. We passed a very pleasant afternoon together. Although I was grateful for the peace, I couldn't bear to think about the next morning.

My mother stayed a little while, after we returned. I don't think she understood what I meant when I told her about Eric's outbursts. I don't honestly think anyone can understand a rage, unless they've witnessed one. The experience is indescribable.

Before bedtime, I prepped Eric for the morning.

"You have an eight o'clock appointment with the psychiatrist, so we'll need to leave here by 7:15. I will wake you up at 7:00 and you will need to get dressed and go right into the car. If you don't, I will call 911 and have you taken to the hospital by ambulance in a straitjacket."

The next morning, a cooperative Eric dressed and went into the car without a problem.

The doctor, a tiny Indian woman, spent an hour with us.

"I feel he is bipolar," she told me.

Finally, a diagnosis!

She handed Eric a lithium prescription. We left the hospital with an appointment for a follow-up visit in a month. I was grateful and relieved, even hopeful we could get our lives back to normal.

The lithium helped. Eric was a little calmer. He wasn't perfect. The anger was still there but the drug took the edge off.

Before long, our trips to the psychiatrist became a battle. Eric didn't want to go. He couldn't stand that she was a woman. She also had a heavy accent, which didn't help.

I thought she was good. She talked to Eric for an hour about his life, what bipolar disorder was, and how to deal with mood swings. During the appointments, he was always polite. In the car, though, the nasty, raging Eric reared his ugly head. He cursed and screamed at me, going to and from the psychiatrist.

After six months, I looked for another doctor.

At that point, for the first time, Eric talked about using drugs. "Mom, I use all different types of drugs," he said, "I even do drugs in school. I just put my head down and snort cocaine in class. The teachers think I'm just sleeping. They're so stupid."

I didn't believe a teacher could be so easily duped. And, why wouldn't they require him to raise his head? It seemed bizarre. Normally, he only told me that type of thing while he raged, so I thought it was a ploy to get me angry, which, in turn, fueled the rage.

Of course, I talked to him about the perils of drug use and how addiction could destroy his life. Of course, I said that if he was using drugs, he needed to stop.

But it didn't make sense to me that a teen would tell his parents he did cocaine, acid, and all sorts of drugs. In my mind, that's something a teenager hides from their parents.

Besides, Eric still wasn't driving during his junior year and when he wasn't at basketball practice, he normally came home right after school. He didn't hang around with upperclassmen that drove, either, except for his girlfriend. How would he even get the drugs?

By the end of his junior year, he worked part time. Before that, though, he subsisted on a ten dollar-a-week allowance. How could he even afford regular drug use? Still, he frequently brought up the topic. I wasn't convinced but I was concerned.

"Maybe, he really is using drugs," I told my husband.

But he disagreed.

"Eric is goading you into a reaction," he said.

I wasn't so sure.

Around that time, Eric verbally attacked me personally. I came to believe his rages allowed him to feel superior to me.

"I am stronger and better than you are!" he said repeatedly, "*You* are weak."

I refused to allow him to think that.

"I am *not* weak. I am a very strong person. A person doesn't have to be physically big and intimidating to be strong," I said, "A person can be strong in other ways."

He gave me a look, as if to say, "You're crazy."

During one episode, he again called me weak.

"My silence is not weakness," I said, "It is silent strength."

He paused, the rage stopped, and he walked away.

I'd been trying hard to not yell back during rages. Tears replaced my screaming and Eric interpreted them as weakness. I didn't cry because I was scared of him. His rages, though unpleasant, had become part of my life.

I cried because, before me, stood a child who was once amazing but, at times, could not control his thoughts and actions, a child I did not recognize. I cried because as his parent, I was supposed to know how to help him. I cried because I was helpless.

9. A Black Eye
Fall 2006

The summer before senior year, Eric lifted weights and attended football practices. When doubles and triples began at the end of August, he was excited. He'd enjoyed the sport during his freshman and sophomore years and, of course, wanted to be quarterback. We all hoped that sitting out junior year hadn't hurt his chances too much.

At the end of the August sessions, he came home after practice one day, beaming, "Mom, I'm the only one being practiced at quarterback, so I think I'm going to be the quarterback!"

He smiled from ear to ear.

"Great, I'm proud of you," I said, "See what can happen when you decide you want something and work hard to get it?"

I hugged him. It was nice seeing him so happy.

Before the school year started, the team held a few scrimmages during, which, none of the three kids vying for quarterback, including Eric, scored a touchdown. The coach decided to start a sophomore as quarterback. The local paper wrote he had decided to 'build for the future.'

As soon as I read the news, it upset me. I didn't like the coaches choosing a sophomore over a senior and I knew Eric would be angry.

After school, one day Eric, Matthew, and I were in the kitchen, when Eric started pacing.

"Everything okay?" I asked, sitting at the table, "Is there something you want to talk about?"

At first, he didn't answer. Then, he screamed.

"The fuckin' coaches are gonna play a sophomore at quarterback! I can't believe it! I worked hard! I was the only one they were practicing at the end of doubles and triples! I thought I was going to be quarterback! I can't believe they're going to play a fuckin' sophomore! It's not fair!"

In his fit, he picked up my car keys from the counter and threw them across the room. They hit me in the face, striking the side of my nose. I couldn't believe my son had physically hurt me. I cried because of, both, the pain and emotional shock. Finally, it had come to this; a physical altercation.

Eric immediately stopped raging and walked over to me.

"Mom, are you okay? I'm sorry. I didn't mean to hit you. I was just so pissed off."

Matthew got ice. I sat, holding it to my face.

"What can I do, Mom?" Eric asked, "I'm sorry. I'm really sorry."

"Leave! Just leave! I can't worry about you right now. Go to a friend's house. Just leave! I can't deal with you right now!"

He hesitated but left.

"Eric keeps calling me to make sure you're okay," Matthew told me. "He is really upset about what happened. I don't think he meant to hit you with the keys."

That night, he slept at a friend's house.

I always told Eric he could lose control of himself when he raged. He always disagreed.

"I would never do physical harm to me or anyone else during these moments," he'd said time and again.

This incident certainly proved me right. It shook up both of us.

When my husband returned from work, he saw me on the couch with a black eye.

"What happened?" he asked.

"Remember Eric thought he had the quarterback position a few days ago? The coaches changed their minds and gave the position to a sophomore," I explained. "Your son was so angry, he screamed about it, picked up my keys, and threw them across the room. They hit me in the face."

He shook his head and walked upstairs. We both knew I couldn't hide my black eye. I believed he was embarrassed that the outside world would see what happened in our house.

I sat on the couch for the next couple of days, extremely upset, nursing my black eye, and bruised mind. I was an emotional wreck.

10. More Often, Peace
Fall 2006–Spring 2007

At back-to-school night of Eric's senior year, I made sure I spoke to Eric's teachers one-on-one in the cafeteria.

They told me he was nice and respectful.

"Eric is a great kid and I love having him in my class!" said his computer skills teacher.

I was thankful my child behaved wonderfully outside the home.

Over and over, I told Eric he was very smart.

"You just need to apply yourself," I said, "You could easily pass all your classes with As or Bs and, probably, without even working too hard."

His reply was always the same.

"Mom, I don't care. I don't like school and I don't need school to make it in this world. Maybe, I was smart when I was younger but that isn't who I am anymore."

"But you're well above average. Your IQ is 142!"

Nothing convinced him of his talent. I couldn't believe a child who excelled in elementary and middle school could lose all that natural talent in only a few years.

He scored 1200 of 1600 on his SATs that year on his first try. I felt the score confirmed my thinking.

"Congratulations, Eric!" I said.

He shrugged off the comment. His score didn't matter to him.

Over time, the lithium he'd been taking for his bipolar disorder had lost its effectiveness for him and his behavior declined.

"I can turn this drug on and off," he told me, "It really isn't helping me."

The new psychiatrist took him off lithium and put him on Risperdal, which worked better. Eric liked her low-key personality. She didn't push him to talk. Once again, I was grateful. I wished she tried harder to engage him but also saw her quiet nature as an asset. He was willing to see her. He complained but pushed back less than when he saw the other psychiatrist.

Mostly, senior year was more of the same; low grades, sports, some rages at home but, more often, peace. *Hopefully*, I thought, *the raging teenage hormones are quieting down.*

Eric got a chance to play varsity basketball that year. Throughout high school, he was point guard; the position of the school superstar. He knew he'd have to wait his turn. He and the other boys did well but they weren't the standouts the school had enjoyed the past three years.

To me and the other parents, that didn't matter; we just wanted to see our sons play.

The varsity coach felt differently. He wanted to win. When the team got behind ten points, he put in freshmen players. I was incensed. With only a ten-point spread, our boys were capable of catching up and, maybe, even, winning the game. They'd waited their turns, only to be replaced by freshmen.

One day Eric came home from school with bombshell news.

"I quit the team today," he said.

"Why would you do that? What happened?"

"Mom, I had to take a stand. The coaches weren't being fair. We waited our turns and then they don't even allow us to play the whole game, most of the time. Sometimes, we're still in the game and they put in freshmen. It's not right, so I just quit. I went to the coach's office and put my uniform on his desk."

"I agree that the coaches weren't right when they wouldn't let you guys play the whole game," I said, "but you still shouldn't have quit. You waited so long to start varsity and you let down the other kids on the team."

Not even his father could change his mind. Deep down, we both knew Eric was right but we'd miss watching him play.

Around that time, Eric insisted on hanging out with his friends, during the week. Sometimes, he went to a friend's house after school. Other times, he drove himself there after dinner. Normally, we didn't let our kids go to friends' houses on weeknights but, tired of the rages, I'd begun to allow it.

Shortly afterwards, I noticed Eric had gained weight. Yet, he didn't seem to be eating more than usual. I concluded he was drinking with his friends and, perhaps, more frequently than just on weekends.

One of his friend's parents had fixed up their garage with a couch and television and allowed the boys to hang out there. I presumed they provided very little supervision, making it easy for Eric and his friends to drink and, possibly, smoke pot regularly.

I spoke to Eric about the dangers of drinking and using drugs.

Again, my warnings fell on deaf ears.

"Mom, marijuana is just like alcohol and alcohol is legal," he'd say, "so, it can't be as bad as they want you to believe."

"If you drink every day because you need a buzz, you're an alcoholic. If you do drugs every day to get a buzz, even if it's marijuana, you're a drug addict."

"Yeah, I get what you're saying," he'd say, "I guess you could be right."

Surprisingly, he didn't always argue with me.

Eric broke his curfew a lot, toward the end of senior year. I tried reining him in but to no avail.

"What are your friends' curfews?" I asked.

"Most of them don't have one," he said.

Not believing him, I called a parent I'd known for years. Lo and behold, her son didn't have a curfew.

I insisted on one, anyway, only to find myself calling Eric at curfew time, demanding that he come home. Staying up past midnight to fight with him over the phone every night drained me. I had to wake up at five every morning for work.

By the end of April, I'd placed Eric in God's hands. I could no longer keep up the vigilance and fighting.

His rages became less frequent and extreme, though, and I spoke to him between episodes. I learned to let him rage and, after he calmed down, return to the topic that upset him. After I said my piece, I quickly walked away, giving him no time to respond.

Much to my surprise, he, sometimes, repeated things I had said. A positive sign. *Is he maturing? Maybe, the teenage hormones are settling down.* Maybe, just maybe, life could get back to normal.

11. Another Diagnosis
Spring 2007

Into the relative, peace came another complication. Eric complained about aches and pains throughout his body. At first, I dismissed them as 'growing pains,' as my mother used to say.

By the middle of senior year, however, it was clear that more was involved.

In the middle of the night, Eric's legs cramped, waking him. He screamed in pain. We rushed into his room to find him massaging his legs, mostly his calves.

My husband brought him a quinine supplement to help the cramping. It didn't work.

Why would a teenage athlete wake up screaming in pain?

After several nights, I brought him to my general practitioner for a physical and blood workup. A few days later, the results surprised us. Eric's liver enzymes were elevated.

"That might indicate Hepatitis B," the doctor said.

"That isn't possible," I replied, "He had the Hepatitis B shots at birth."

"Let's stay calm," he told me, "We need to do some follow-up blood work to confirm the possible diagnosis."

Two weeks later, we knew, Eric had Hepatitis B.

I couldn't believe it. He was one of the first babies in South Korea to be inoculated against the virus. This was not supposed to happen.

A third and definitive test was done with the same result. Eric had more than a hundred million viruses per milliliter of blood, the equivalent of approximately twenty drops.

After he went on medication, he didn't wake up in pain anymore.

Now I had a child with a birth mother, who had bestowed him with mental illness and hepatitis B. He had two reasons to be angry with her and, of course, direct that anger at me.

We began Eric's treatment for hepatitis at a teaching hospital in a nearby city. Not wanting to go to yet another doctor, Eric cursed every mile to and from our appointments.

"With proper treatment, you can live to be an old man," I said, "You can marry, have a family, and experience all the things you have planned."

The encouragement did not help.

"Why do I have to deal with another fuckin' problem!" he cried out.

One day, when I returned home from work, I found him at the computer.

"I'm looking up information on Hepatitis B," he said. "Do you know there's only a four percent chance I could get the virus from my birth mother after receiving the shots? What the hell! I can't believe there's only a four percent chance and it happens to me."

He screamed and resisted taking his medicine, which his liver doctor could not understand. He wasn't sympathetic to the tightrope I walked or Eric's emotional issues. Often, he was terse with Eric and, sometimes, with me.

I couldn't blame him. Yet, he wasn't hearing my story.

He was not hearing that his patient was mentally ill and that taking medicine was mentally difficult for him.

The raw truth was that Eric would rather be dead.

At that point in his life, death appealed to him. He often talked about killing himself. He knew he was in pain. He also knew he caused me a lot of pain. He knew he was often not a good son and, sometimes, thought that if he were dead, everyone's life would be much easier.

The hepatologist might have been great but he wasn't right for my son. After nine months, I found a new one.

12. Graduating High School
June 2007

I worried Eric would do something unexpected and embarrassing at his High School graduation, an event that saddened me. My amazing child with an IQ of 142, once filled with promise, received mostly Cs, Ds, and Fs, throughout his high school career. He graduated near the bottom of his class.

His father and I did not take his grades lightly. We'd encouraged him to take his studies seriously.

During his sophomore year, I insisted that he study at the dining room table for at least an hour each day. In the beginning, he sat though he wouldn't always study. Eventually, he raged.

I reminded him to study when I knew a test was scheduled. Sometimes, I spoke to his teachers to see what assignments he was missing and what projects were coming up.

He met all my efforts with lots of resistance.

During his senior year, after speaking to his English teacher, I discovered he was supposed to read the book, *Entertaining an Elephant*, and write a report about it.

"I have no intention of reading it," he said. "I can pass the class without doing the assignment."

Unconvinced, I read the book with him. We took turns reading the chapters and discussed the story. He did the report and received a passing grade.

I knew I shouldn't have to involve myself in my child's schoolwork to that extent. Not at that stage but I was still determined to drive home the importance of doing what was expected of him, even if he didn't want to do it.

He often told me *Entertaining an Elephant* was his favorite book.

Not until graduation, did I fully lament the would-have-beens, should-have-beens, and could-have-beens. I looked back over the life of my child, who, perhaps, could not use his innate talents because of the madness that took over his mind in High School. It had all been wasted. Was that a conscious choice? Or due to mental illness? It didn't matter. I had to come to terms with the fact that my son was no longer amazing.

I couldn't help but think about where he could have graduated in his class, if he'd just made different choices or used his God-given abilities. I would love to have been born with his brain.

I always envisioned my son at the top of his class, possibly as the scholar-athlete or valedictorian or salutatorian. Even if he didn't achieve such a title, I saw him giving those who did a run for their money.

Instead, Eric was content to be near the bottom, to blow off life, and to take it one day at a time. He did not plan or think about the future because he didn't think he had one.

"Mom, I'll be dead by the time I'm twenty-two," he frequently told me.

13. The New Eric
Fall 2007

The summer after high school, Eric worked two jobs at a local restaurant and golf course and made a lot of tips.

I was glad to see him responsibly getting up and out of the house on his own.

We were always good savers, so we encouraged Eric to do the same. He told us he'd opened a bank account and was saving money. When I went into our local branch, the ladies who worked there commented on Eric.

"I love it when he comes to the bank," one teller effused.

"So do I," said another, "He always has a smile on his face. He makes me laugh."

The news cheered me. Eric really was saving money, which might mean he thought he had a future, after all.

While he worked that summer, he also drank and smoked pot regularly with his friends. Most nights, Eric worked until eleven at night and then saw his friends.

On one rare occasion when he was home, I questioned him.

"Why do you have to go out *every* night to see your friends? It'd be good if you'd come home directly from work sometimes and stay home. Working all day and going out every night until one in the morning, you're going to get sick."

"Mom, my friends are the most important things in my life," he replied, "I need to hang out with them as much as possible."

"But what about spending time with us?"

"You guys are important, Mom, but not as important as my friends."

I was hurt and insulted but not surprised.

"In life, friends move away and go their separate ways," I said, "You might keep in touch but your family will always be there for you."

He shook his head, rolled his eyes, and laughed.

"No, not for me and my friends, Mom. We will *always* be close and they will *always* be the most important things to me. Sorry, but my family will *never* be as important as my friends."

His words stung me but I brushed them off.

"Make sure you're home by one when you go out," I said.

Eventually, one o'clock in the morning became two, then three. As the summer wore on, he often didn't come home at all.

At first, I worried. I frantically called his cell phone to see where he was. He told me he crashed at friends' houses a lot, so he didn't drive after drinking. After a time, I assumed that's why he didn't come home. I was glad he kept himself off the road but I still didn't understand why he and his friends had to drink every night.

When I encouraged Eric to invite his friends over, he refused.

"They don't want to hang out here," he said.

Again, I was insulted but I knew why. We had rules. There was no place for them to hide in our house and we wouldn't let them drink or smoke pot.

I didn't like the direction Eric's life was taking but I wasn't sure what to do. If I said too much, we argued and a rage could surface. So, I constantly talked to him about drug use, drinking too much, and making good choices, when he was receptive.

I also constantly told him I loved him. Sometimes, I thought he was listening. Other times, I knew he wasn't.

He'd enrolled in community college for the fall, so I prayed the partying and late nights would end in September.

Late in August, Eric sheepishly approached me.

"I really don't want to go to community college, Mom."

"Eric, you should try college. You may find something that interests you and you know getting a good-paying job with only a high school diploma won't be easy. You need college or trade school."

"I don't know, Mom. I don't see why I need a college degree. I can make it in life without one. You know I only agreed to go for you and Dad. I really never wanted to go."

"Your father and I feel you should give college a chance," I continued abruptly, "You need to make up your mind, though, because I don't want you wasting our money."

After Labor Day, Eric settled down, started college, and suffered a severe bout of depression. One Saturday morning he slept through his alarm, missing his shift at the golf course. Knowing he had to work, I tried to wake him.

"Shut up and leave me alone!" he screamed.

He couldn't move.

His boss called the house.

"Where is he?" he asked.

"He's not feeling well. I'm sorry he didn't call you but I wasn't home," I said, "He must have slept through his alarm."

The next day was more of the same as Eric lay on the futon in our basement.

Again, his boss called.

"I'm concerned," he said, "Is Eric coming in today?"

I was near tears because I didn't know what to say. When I tried waking Eric, he screamed.

"Eric suffers from depression," I told his boss. I didn't know what else to say. "I'm so sorry. I will have him call you when he feels better."

On Monday, Eric moved. When he walked into the kitchen, I bombarded him with questions.

"How are you feeling? You have me very worried. What's wrong? Do you want me to take you to the doctor?"

He waved me away.

"No, no, no," he said, shaking his head, "I don't need a doctor."

"Do you want to try therapy again? It might be good to talk about things. You know depression goes along with bipolar disorder, so therapy might help."

"No, no," he repeated, "I don't need therapy. I just wasn't feeling good, that's all. I'm fine now."

I remained unconvinced.

"Alright. Let me know if you change your mind. I can always make a doctor or therapy appointment for you. Oh, call your boss from the golf course. He's been calling. He's very worried about you, like I am."

He never called his boss.

By the end of September, I'd come to the sad conclusion my amazing son may very well die at a very young age. The constant late nights and drinking and drugs, along with his not caring about the future, were a recipe for disaster.

The thought of burying him brought me to tears.

For a few years, he'd been telling me his life would be short and he had to 'live it to the fullest.'

"Living life to the fullest means using all your God-given talents," I said, "Partying every night is wasting your life."

I still believed he was drinking and smoking pot, not doing harder drugs.

As September gave way to October, I came to the horrible realization that I had, in a sense, already buried Eric. My son, the amazing boy I raised, was already dead. The little boy I took so much time to care for, encourage, and love, no longer existed. He'd been curious. He'd loved to learn. He had plans for the future.

He was gone.

The child I faced everyday had no interest in learning or even living.

The realization depressed me. For the next few weeks, I pushed myself through each day. I went to work and cared for my family in a daze, putting on a happy face for the outside world, even though I felt broken inside. *How in the world did this happen?*

Through the depressing fog that enveloped me, I made a decision. I had to learn to love the new Eric. Although, I didn't agree with his decisions and felt he was wasting his potential, I had to accept the person he'd become. After all, he was my son and I would always love him.

I knew acceptance would be difficult. Deep down, I wanted to believe he was still capable of great things.

14. Ground Rules
Fall 2007

As fall semester started, I went over Eric's college syllabi with him. I offered to buy him a calendar, so he could plan the start of long-term assignments. I asked what type of papers he'd have to write. I asked how often he'd have tests in each class. I offered my assistance.

His initial enthusiasm waned quickly. He completed assignments, when he did them, an hour or two before class.

"Eric, you've *got* to plan your time," I implored him. "You can do this. You can be successful at school."

"No Mom, I can't," he replied, "I'm not as smart as you think that I am. I have a hard time concentrating and remembering things."

"No, Eric, you are very smart. You just need to apply and organize yourself. You need to plan time for studying into your busy schedule. You are very smart and you need to begin to believe that."

It was to no avail.

At the end of October, I found out Eric and his friends were doing hard drugs. The news devastated me.

I realized all the late nights and constant partying must stop before he or one of his friends got hurt or killed. So, I called the parents of some of his friends.

The first one was very receptive and suggested a group of us meet for dinner.

I saw a second parent at a football game and spoke to her through tears.

"They are partying too much," she said, "I'm okay with setting some ground rules."

The third parent I called agreed to meet for dinner.

"But there's no way my son does hard drugs," she insisted.

"I'm not so sure about that," I told her, "They all hang out together and I doubt your son just sits and watches everyone else do drugs."

My statement upset her. After we hung up, she called her son, who, in turn, called Eric.

My phone rang.

"Why did you call Tom's mother?" Eric screamed on the other end, "What did you say to get her so upset? She just called Tom crying. Why are you even getting involved?"

"I heard you and your friends are doing hard drugs," I said, "I cannot and will not watch you all destroy yourselves."

"You should mind your own business," Eric countered, "How dare you tell on my friends!"

"I am not 'telling on' your friends, Eric. I'm trying to stop something bad from happening. I'm worried about you and your friends. What if one of you gets hurt because of drugs or, worse yet, dies? What if my becoming involved stops something horrible from happening? I can't keep this type of information to myself. I wouldn't be able to live with myself, if something happened to one of you because I didn't do something to stop your destructive behavior."

He became very quiet.

"I understand, Mom, I understand," he said calmly, "I've got to get back to work. I'll talk to you later."

With that, he hung up.

His calm demeanor shocked me. He had showed some maturity and seemed to understand my point of view.

At our dinner, we mothers decided on a one o'clock curfew and a ban on sleepovers during the week. Life became a little more predictable and peaceful for a time.

Eric ended his first semester at community college with three Fs and two Ds. He didn't want to return to school in January.

I wanted him to stay in college but not if he didn't apply himself.

"You don't have to continue," I said, "But you have to find a full-time job that gives you health benefits, at some point."

As a full-time student, he could stay on our health plan. Once he lost his student status, we had to pay for his insurance benefits. My husband's plan extended him an individual policy for a reasonable price.

Eric needed health coverage. His Hepatitis medicine cost $825 per month and his medication for bipolar disorder, $400 per month. We couldn't cover those costs long-term.

15. Light at the End of the Tunnel
2008

Insisting he was okay, Eric stopped going to the psychiatrist and taking medicine for bipolar disorder.

Although, still scary and volatile at times, he raged less frequently and severely. I was grateful but feared how he might behave without meds. I wasn't sure he could control himself but what were my options? I certainly couldn't stuff the pills down his throat.

I accepted we'd have an un-medicated, mentally ill child around the house.

Around that time, we found a new liver specialist, who understood Eric's issues and my difficulties. She treated Eric respectfully at each visit. He really liked her. She was thorough and educated both of us about the disease.

The drives to see his new doctor were calm; a nice change of pace. We made the appointments for late in the day, so I could meet him at a halfway point after work and go with him. I wasn't sure he'd get there himself. Also, I wanted to know what was going on with my son.

His viral levels had gone down considerably from the starting number of more than one hundred million viruses per milliliter of blood but they weren't at zero, which was what the doctor had expected.

She questioned him about Baraclude, a medicine he had to take one hour before or three hours after he ate. He admitted he sometimes forgot to take it because of the difficult timing.

"Remember that there are only three or four medications that work for Hepatitis B," the doctor said. "We don't want the virus to mutate and become resistant to the available drugs."

He promised to do better and I reminded him but he still jumped into his clothes and ran out of the house in the mornings to get to work on time, often without taking his medicine.

Sleeping had become a problem for him. He worked most nights and came home around ten thirty. If he went out with his friends, he came home by the one o'clock curfew and roamed the house for hours, making himself something to eat, cleaning his room, and doing laundry in the middle of the night.

He made a lot of noise, disturbing my sleep. Afraid he might fall asleep while cooking and burn down the house, I dragged myself out of bed and down the stairs, when the cooking smell became strong. I had to make sure everything was okay.

When I was younger, I worked nights at a restaurant so I understood that when you get home late, you need time to unwind, maybe sit and have a small snack. Eric was eating a meal, though, not a snack.

Usually, he fell asleep in the basement to the sound of the television.

I spoke to him about these bad habits but it didn't help. Eric just could not sleep.

We saw the liver specialist every three months. Eric had to go for blood work two to three weeks before his appointment. It took about two weeks to get the test results to check his viral levels. I went to the lab with him whenever I could but our conflicting schedules sometimes made that impossible. He worked early afternoons into the night. I left the house at 6:15 in the morning and got home around three or four o'clock in the afternoon.

A couple of times when we went to the liver specialist, the lab results were not there. At first, I was certain the lab had lost them. I called and had them check their records.

As time passed, I realized Eric had not been going to the lab. Later, he admitted that if they were busy when he arrived, he just left and forgot to go back. I couldn't believe he could be so irresponsible. He still didn't comprehend the importance of taking care of himself.

After a while, I accompanied him to the lab on weekends.

As his viral levels declined, his behavior improved. This improvement continued even after he stopped taking his medication for bipolar disorder. He raged less and, when he had an episode, it was much less severe.

I questioned whether the high viral levels in his blood may have had something to do with his bizarre behavior.

When Eric was seeing the second psychiatrist, I had asked that very question. She explained Hepatitis B has caused depression in some patients. But the liver specialist said she hadn't seen any studies on the topic. The conflict of information between the two doctors confused me. I could not help but see a connection between the two conditions.

In researching on my own, I discovered approximately twenty percent of those with Hepatitis B and the HIV virus also suffered from mental illness. According to prevailing thought, a mentally ill person is more likely to engage in risky behaviors that lead to contracting such a virus.

I started to wonder if the researchers had it backwards. *What if high levels of a virus in a person's bloodstream cause them to behave in a manner consistent with mental illness?*

Eric had more than one hundred million viruses per milliliter of blood in his system. What if the virus had gotten into his brain? Would it have interrupted the smooth transport of neurotransmitters between neurons required for good mental health?

To answer this question, I needed to know if the Hepatitis B virus could cross the blood-brain barrier. Not an easy thing to find out. Even the scientific literature at a local college failed to produce an answer.

A nurse friend offered to ask a colleague, who worked for a liver specialist. The colleague, also a nurse, said the Hepatitis B virus is capable of crossing the blood-brain barrier and is known to cause depression and even, psychosis.

The psychiatrist, who treated Eric, had acknowledged a possible connection that his two liver specialists couldn't confirm. I wondered, *Why the disconnect between the liver and psychiatric communities?*

In the meantime, life definitely calmed down. Eric often worked ten- to twelve-hour days as a cook and seemed to save money. He appeared to be more responsible.

A new girlfriend in his life also bolstered him. Once Eric introduced her to us, she went out of her way to talk with me. I appreciated her friendliness. They got along well and Eric seemed very happy.

"Mom, would it be okay if I married her?" he asked me one day, when she was at the house.

"I have no problem with your getting married," I replied, "But I do have a problem with the timing. You two need to get more settled first. You both have to get higher-paying jobs and one needs to offer health benefits."

During this time, Eric was promoted from pizza delivery driver to cook and discovered a passion for cooking. He loved it so much that he talked about going to culinary school.

Overall, I saw the new developments as positive signs. Life in the Burns household for the next nine months was more peaceful than it had been for a very long time.

I even thought, *Maybe Eric would live past twenty-two and have a future.*

They say that when things appear better, you can see 'the light at the end of the tunnel.' I thought I saw a light and I thought it was at the end of the tunnel.

I was wrong.

The light was from a train headed in my direction; a train that flattened me, a train I didn't expect.

16. "I Need Help"
Summer 2009

Eric walked out of the house as I weeded the front yard garden. He stood on the walkway. I looked up, squinting in the sun.

"Mom, I need to tell you something."

I stood.

"Okay, I'm listening," I said, wiping the sweat from my brow, "What is it?"

"You need to come inside and sit down for this."

He lowered his eyes, turned around, and walked back into the house. I put down my trowel, snapped off my gardening gloves, and followed him to the family room. With life going so well, what horrible news could he possibly have?

I sat on the couch. He stood in front of me. He seemed nervous.

"Mom, I need help," he said, "I've become addicted to drugs."

I looked at him, unable to respond.

"I'm addicted to OxyContin, Mom. I need help. I don't want to be addicted anymore."

He shifted his weight, stared at the floor, and shook his head.

I was unable to move. I was shocked. I couldn't believe what I was hearing. He and his friends partied more often than they should but for the past six months, he'd been working fifty-plus hours a week and performing extremely well. How could he be so functional and addicted to drugs?

"Of course I'll help you," I said, "I'm not sure what to do but I'll get you the help you need."

A few minutes later I lifted myself off the couch and headed straight for the phone in the kitchen.

"What do I do?" I asked my nurse friend.

"Take him to a hospital with a detox unit," she said, giving me a name.

After I hung up, I stared at the information I'd just written. I cried. I'd really thought we were over the worst.

Next, I arranged for a colleague at work to give one of my classes its final exam. I knew I shouldn't miss any days during the last week of school but I had to. I had to take care of my son. I had to try to save Eric.

We left for the hospital after dinner. The ride was quiet.

"Mom, I'm sorry," he said.

I couldn't hide how upset I was. Eric and I had been through a lot, but this? *This might be bigger than both of us.* Thinking about the future frightened me. Drug addiction is very scary. Drugs destroy people. Drugs destroy lives. Drugs are difficult to leave behind. A drug addiction is often inescapable.

I parked in the hospital lot. Not knowing what to expect, we walked into the emergency room. As Eric described his addiction to the doctor, his words pained me.

"OxyContin," he said, "Two half-pills a day. Maybe, three."

At the end of that horrible night, he came home. His addiction was not severe enough to admit him.

Never did I dream they'd turn us away.

Never could I have imagined my son writhing in pain on the couch in our home as I entered the maze of addiction treatment by myself with no guide. I didn't know how to detox a patient. I didn't know where to begin. All I knew was I had to get help.

I started with an 800 number in the yellow pages.

Through tears, I told the man who answered of our hospital visit. I told him Eric was trying to detox at home. He was understanding, helpful, and incredulous the hospital hadn't admitted my son.

"Even if he could detox at home, he needs to attend an inpatient rehab program to become drug free," he said, "If you can get him to California, we'll get approval from your insurance company for a thirty-day stay here."

California? I wasn't sure about sending Eric that far away.

A local rehab place gave me a different story. The insurance company would not allow Eric into an inpatient rehab, unless he'd first been through an outpatient rehab program. I was convinced Eric needed inpatient rehab; though, I certainly didn't want the $20,000 price tag that came with it.

Next, I called the insurance company, which confirmed what the local rehab had said. *Why could a California rehab get the insurance company to pay for thirty days but a local one couldn't?* Needing to make a decision fast, my husband and I opted for outpatient rehab.

I choose a program forty minutes away in another county, figuring Eric would make new local friends with drug problems at a closer facility.

After one day of detoxing, Eric went back to work. He arrived late a pizzeria, saying he didn't feel good but could manage and work through the pain. When business at the restaurant was slow, his boss let him rest. I called throughout the day to check on him.

The eight-week outpatient program, which started early in July, required Eric to take a leave of absence from his job. After he registered, Eric gave his boss notice. He attended three meetings a week. Each began as a large group discussion of a particular topic and then broke into smaller groups for more intimate conversation.

Once a week, he was supposed to get individual therapy. Once a week, he was drug tested. If he failed the test, he'd be booted from the program.

Eric was very good about going and never complained. When he arrived home after each meeting, he calmly told me what he learned that day, giving lots of detail, and showing me any written material he had received.

His ability to retain so much information impressed me. I felt relief. My son was getting the help he needed.

Toward the end of the program, he had a minor car accident, after which, I drove him to and from the meetings. When I dropped him off, I saw him join the rest of the attendees at the front door with a genuine sense of familiarity.

But I was unhappy he only had two or three individual therapy sessions. I wasn't sure why and prompted Eric to schedule an appointment. He didn't. For some reason, I didn't understand, he seemed averse to therapy.

Eric was a young man with a severe problem. Why wouldn't he want to understand how he became addicted, how drugs impacted his life, and how to overcome them? I thought talking to someone would help him feel more in control. Unfortunately, Eric did not see things that way.

During the program, the adoption issue raised its head again.

"Mom," he asked, "Please call the adoption agency and see if my birth mother was an addict, when she delivered me."

Also curious, I called the adoption agency. What I discovered disturbed me.

No, his birth mother hadn't been a drug addict but nine months before the birth she'd been gang raped.

"She and a friend went to Pusan, where they met three or four young men around the age of twenty-five," the agency representative said, "They raped Eric's birth mother."

That was the story on paper, anyway. Was she really raped? Or did she have consensual sex with strangers and say she was raped once she found herself pregnant and, perhaps, afraid and ashamed? Either scenario is possible.

If she was raped, though, Eric was conceived at a time of extreme stress and violence. His father, by the sheer definition of rape, was violent.

Did that difficult conception help explain Eric's violent rages? What so tormented my son? His past and his inner life were an ever-deepening mystery.

17. A November Storm
Fall 2009

After Eric finished outpatient therapy, he didn't return to the pizzeria. I didn't know why but I supported his decision to start over. A new job would help.

At that point, I was convinced he really couldn't concentrate. For the past year, the Hepatitis B levels in his bloodstream had decreased. If my hypothesis was correct and the viruses had gotten into his brain, maybe he really couldn't meet the demands of academics. Maybe, that's why he did so poorly in High School.

His viral levels were nowhere near the sky-high numbers of the previous fall but, maybe, his brain needed time to heal. A year of drinking and drugging surely had affected his brain as well.

I found many reasons for optimism. He'd also been drug free all eight weeks of outpatient rehab and, over the past nine months, his behavior had steadily improved.

When Eric renewed his enthusiasm for community college, we agreed to pay for one more semester. He registered.

When September came, he was still dating the same girl. He landed a job at a diner thirty minutes from home. I was glad he worked in another county and hoped he'd make new friends, who didn't party every night.

He still went out with his old friends after his shift, though, albeit, not as often. He still slept poorly, too, and cooked in the middle of the night.

Overall, though, life was much calmer.

But his schoolwork concerned me. I didn't see him study much. I could only hope he studied while I was at work.

"You want out of this boring life you think we live, Eric?" I confronted him, "School is your ticket."

But he couldn't motivate himself.

In October, my family threw me a surprise fiftieth birthday party. Jessica and Eric planned the event and Eric did a lot of the cooking. Jessica made appetizers and Eric, the main dishes. The two of them told me they worked all day.

"Eric was in charge, Mom," Jessica said, "He calmed me down when I was overwhelmed."

Eric, the calm one? I found that amusing.

That night Eric hugged me many times.

"I love you, Mom! Happy birthday!" he said.

After most guests left, I opened my gifts; many nice items along with a couple of fifty-dollar bills, one, of which, disappeared by morning.

By the end of October, Eric fell back into bad habits. He worked and went to school but he also went out every night and overslept in the mornings. I was certain he wasn't studying. I talked to him about his habits but to no avail.

That fall, my diamond earrings and one gold necklace disappeared.

"Eric, did you take any of my jewelry?" I asked.

He denied it.

My husband noticed some of his coins were missing. Again, we questioned Eric.

"I take a roll occasionally," he said, "But not all of them."

A few months earlier, I had misplaced my Exxon credit card. I never canceled it because I was sure I'd find it. When the next monthly bill showed $738 due, I was annoyed at myself but mostly at Eric. I was sure he'd made the charges, which showed many small purchases in gas station marts located on his way to school or near his girlfriend's house.

He denied making the charges but his lying was obvious. Eric had become a prolific liar.

Though extremely upset with him, I was amazed that he apparently never anticipated that such a large bill would raise our suspicions.

When we determined Eric and his friends spent too much money on drugs and alcohol, we charged him $200 a week to live at home, starting in January. Since he was working full-time, we told him, he could help pay bills.

Instead of using the money to pay bills, though, we opened up a bank account for Eric, so he'd have money for a new car, when he needed one. His 2002 black Hyundai had high mileage.

One day, my husband slipped and told Eric what we were doing with his weekly rent.

In the beginning, he gave us the money willingly. Then, I had to ask him for it. If he didn't have it, he got nasty with me.

When he stopped giving me rent altogether, I knew something was wrong.

November came in like a storm. Eric's anger worsened. During the first week, I called my husband at work twice and asked him to come home. I couldn't handle Eric's drug addiction alone, anymore.

The first time he came home, he talked to Eric and calmed him down.

The second time, at Eric's request, he accompanied us to the psychiatrist's office. During the appointment, Eric admitted to the Exxon charges and to stealing my earrings. We discussed his anger.

He denied using drugs, though I was convinced they'd become a problem again.

Nevertheless, I left grateful. Finally, I had a confession and a prescription to help Eric control himself. Yet, in my heart, I knew he'd need rehab again.

In the days that followed our family meeting with the psychiatrist, I felt sick to my stomach. I researched inpatient programs and jotted down names of a few places that sounded good. I also braced myself, knowing I'd have to confront Eric, put up with his raging anger, and send him away. It was only a matter of time.

It didn't take long. On Saturday, November 7, Eric stormed into the house, very agitated.

"Mom, give me my money," he demanded.

"What money are you talking about?"

"My money, the money I've been giving you every week as rent. I need it. Give it to me now."

"You can't have it," I replied, trying to stay calm, "It's for a car."

"It's *my* money!" He screamed, "You need to give it to me. You need to give it to me *now*! I don't need to worry about a new car. My car is going to last forever!"

"Your car isn't going to last forever. That money is for a car and nothing else."

He continued to scream and paced back and forth in the kitchen.

"I need the money! You have no right to keep it! It is my fuckin' money! You need to give it to me *now*!"

I held my ground.

"I will not give you the money. It is not your money. It is rent that you have been paying us for living here," I said, "We are just being nice by putting it in an account, so you'll have it for a new car."

"I don't need a fuckin' new car!"

He ran out of the house, screaming.

"I'll go to the bank then and demand that they give me my money."

I ran after him.

"Don't you dare go into the bank and scream at the people who work there," I yelled back, "They will not be able to give you that money. It's in an account in my name."

He stopped, turned around, and glared at me.

"You have until tomorrow to get the money out of the bank and give it to me," he sneered. "If you don't, you'll be sorry."

I knew he'd use the money for drugs, so I held my ground.

"I will not give it to you."

"Then, you'll be sorry!"

I called the police.

They arrived. This time Eric did not calm down. He was angry. He was in pain. He needed drugs. The police talked to him but he screamed at them and cursed them, while pacing the front yard.

"She won't give me money that's mine," he told the officers, "She has no right to keep my money."

The officers carefully tried to engage him.

"What do you need the money for?" one asked.

"What the fuck! That's none of your business. I don't have to tell anyone what I'm going to use my money for."

Much to my amazement, I leaned against the front door of the house and watched the scene unfold very calmly. I couldn't believe what I saw. *Am I watching a movie? How can this be my son? My life?*

"He's addicted to drugs and he is demanding that I give him money for drugs and I refused to give him any money," I told the officers, "He needs to go to detox."

"We can call an ambulance to bring him to the hospital, if you think he'll go willingly," one officer offered.

I wasn't sure.

"Eric, you have to go to the hospital," I yelled out to him, "You have to detox and get the help you need."

"I'll go but only if you drive me," he screamed, still pacing, "I won't go in an ambulance."

I agreed to drive him. The police left.

At that point, Eric was angry, raging, and very scary. I was mentally and emotionally worn out. The thought of driving him thirty minutes to a hospital in his condition unnerved me. I didn't want to be alone with him in the car, so I asked Matthew to ride with us.

Thankfully, the ride was quiet. Eric sat in the front seat, Matthew in the back.

I didn't look at Eric or say a word. Though my insides were shaking, I stayed composed and focused on the road.

As we got closer to the hospital, Eric made some phone calls. By the time we arrived, he'd arranged for a friend to pick him up.

"You've just wasted your time driving me here," he said, "I'm not going in."

When I pulled up in front of the hospital, I glared at him and held out his insurance card.

"You need help. You cannot live at home unless you go through detox and then to a rehab program," I said, "You cannot be addicted to drugs and live at home anymore."

He glared back at me, grabbed the card from my hand, got out of the car, and slammed the door.

I drove away.

By the time I returned home, I was an emotional mess. I called my husband and told him what had just happened. Then, I called one of Eric's friends and asked him to help me. I told him Eric needed rehab.

"Maybe, you can talk him into getting the help he needs."

"I've been concerned for Eric for a while, Mrs. Burns," he said, "A month ago, I tried taking him to the local inpatient rehab but they couldn't admit him due to insurance. I'll talk to him again."

Four months earlier, the same rehab told me Eric had to first go through an outpatient program. He had! So why was he turned away?

After I hung up, I left the house. Eric was bound to come back for his belongings and I refused to be there, when he did. I refused to argue with him again.

I called one of my sisters but she didn't pick up her phone. I *really* needed to go somewhere so I could cry like a baby. I wasn't sure where, so I drove around aimlessly, stopping in stores and meandering the aisles; a feeble attempt to keep my mind off the horror I'd just endured.

I felt sick and exhausted but how I felt didn't matter. I knew I couldn't go home.

At one point, it dawned on me I must look like a train wreck to my fellow shoppers. After all, I'd just fought with an angry teenager in need of a fix, called the police, drove my son to detox, and kicked him out the house. I quickly decided I didn't care what other people thought. I was allowed to look like a train wreck.

Two hours later, I called home. Jessica picked up the phone. She was crying. A sick feeling came over me.

"What's the matter?"

"Eric just left. He came home to get some of his things and said goodbye to me and Matthew," she said, "He said he didn't know when he would see us again. What's going to happen to him?"

I couldn't console her. I didn't know what would happen to Eric.

18. Texas

November 2009

Eric's friends staged an intervention that very evening. The next morning, he called me from the hospital.

"Mom, I'm at the hospital and they're not going to help me again," he said, sounding frustrated, "No one's going to help me."

"Where are you?" I asked.

"My friends took me to where you brought me in June and they won't admit me. They told me that my drug habit isn't bad enough and the insurance company won't approve my being admitted again."

I stood in the kitchen, leaning on the island counter, not believing what I heard. How bad does someone's drug habit have to be in New Jersey before their insurance company will pay for detox?

"I thought we might get to this point," I said, "Last week, I looked up some out-of-state inpatient rehabs. I can call them to see if they have a bed available, if you're willing to go."

"Yeah, Mom, I'll go."

"Okay, I'll call you back and let you know if I find a bed."

"Okay," he hesitated, "Mom, I'm sorry."

I hung up the phone and started dialing with confidence. Our insurance company *would* pay for an out-of-state inpatient rehab but not for a detox unit. Why? I wasn't sure but it didn't matter. I just wanted to get my son the help he needed.

The places I chose were far away. I didn't want to make it easy for Eric to find his way home via bus, train, or hitchhiking. I didn't want him so close that a friend could easily pick him up or send him enough money to get home. At twenty years old, Eric was very aware he could sign himself out of a rehab facility at any time.

The first place I called didn't take any insurance.

The second place took ours and it had an available bed. My out-of-pocket expense would be around fourteen hundred dollars. That figure was manageable.

Eric called me back and I told him our good fortune. He agreed to come home and get ready to leave. I immediately booked him on an eight o'clock flight that very evening.

Once Eric arrived home, we went to a local store. I bought him toothpaste, shampoo, and deodorant along with snacks, including granola bars, beef jerky, and gum. I also broke down and bought a carton of cigarettes; that purchase killed me, since I hated that he smoked.

After returning home, we took the largest suitcase we owned out of the attic and packed it together in his room. I gave him fifty dollars, even though I wasn't sure he'd need any money.

As we packed, I had time to think about what was happening. I wasn't sure how I felt. I was happy my son finally would get the help I thought he needed. Yet, I also was helping him pack for a one-month drug rehab.

We left for the airport around five o'clock. Jessica came along. I was grateful for her company. The ride was very quiet.

We entered the terminal, checked his bag, and walked Eric to security. Before he went through, he hugged me.

"Mom, I'm sorry. I'm really sorry. I love you."

I hugged him back.

"I love you, too, and I need you to get better," I said through tears, "Please, get better. I want you back."

I stood for a few moments, unable to move, and watched him go through security. Jessica snapped me out of my trance.

"Mom, Mom, let's go," she said.

Still frozen and unable to speak, I looked at her.

"Come on," she said, taking me by the arm and walking me out.

Eric arrived in San Antonio, Texas around midnight. An employee from the rehab picked him up at the airport.

Though I was a wreck, I went to work the next day. I stayed close to my classroom and focused on what I had to do. Most of the day, I was close to tears. When I wasn't teaching, I was crying in my room.

Some of my colleagues knew about Eric. One told me to enjoy the month because it'd be the most peaceful I'd have for a long time. He'd been in my shoes.

At the rehab, Eric was put in detox for four days. He had phone privileges immediately, however, and called me screaming.

"Mom, you need to let me come home. These people aren't doing anything to help me. The food is horrible and all they talk about is God."

"You can't come home. You need to get better," I said, "You need to stay there and get the help you need so you're no longer addicted. Remember, you can't live at home, if you're addicted."

"Mom, I don't fuckin' need to be here! Please let me come home. Really, this place isn't going to help me."

He cursed and swore at me. He begged me. I wasn't sure what to think. I'd sent my son to a rehab, sight unseen, more than a thousand miles away. Did I make the right decision?

Eric called constantly. After a couple of days, I refused to pick up the phone. Finally, I unplugged it. I could no longer handle the anger. I was tired of his abuse.

I called his counselor. She listened. I learned most people who end up in rehab go through this scenario. I felt much better. After our conversation, I was confident Eric was in a good place with good people, who would try to help him.

"But when he calls, he screams and curses at me," I told her, "If that's how he's going to speak to me, I don't want him calling at all."

We agreed that, until he settled in, he could only call me from her office. A couple of hours later, the phone rang.

"Hi, Mom," Eric said, "I'm calling from my counselor's office. I'm sorry about calling you so much and giving you such a hard time."

"Yeah, you can't call and scream at me. I won't have you talking to me like that anymore. I'm tired of the nonsense. I know this isn't easy for you but I really need you to get better. I need you to be healthy, so you can come home."

"I know, Mom, I know. I'm going to try. I really am. I love you."

"I love you, too."

Once he settled in, Eric thrived. He grew close to his counselor and talked to her after his small group therapy session. He also made good friends and, during free afternoon time, played basketball or volleyball with kids his age.

In no time, Eric called me in a happy mood.

"I'm having a great time," he said, "I'm amazed at how much fun I can have without being high."

The old Eric was returning.

The rehab invited us to a family weekend to learn about drug addiction and how we could support our recovering addict when he returned home. My husband and I went. Jessica and Matthew also wanted to go but four flights were just too expensive.

We arrived in San Antonio late on a Thursday night and drove an hour to the rehab facility the next morning. I thought of how scared Eric must have been the night he arrived but, somehow, I couldn't feel sorry for him.

After we signed in, we found Eric, who seemed genuinely glad to see us. His counselor came to meet us on her day off. She ushered us into her office, where we discussed Eric's progress.

We listened to Eric talk about his drug habit and what he'd done in active addiction. Horrified, I listened.

"How could you think to do that?" I burst out, "Why would you think that was okay?"

His counselor quickly interjected.

"Just listen," the counselor told me, "If you react like that, you'll lose him."

I calmed down but wished someone had told me to expect such a confession. After our meeting, Eric showed us around and introduced us to his new friends, who called him 'Jersey.' Clearly, he was well-liked.

Throughout the day, patients and families went to their respective meetings. We visited Eric for short periods, during breaks. The days were warm and sunny, so, during the afternoon break, I sat outside and watched Eric play volleyball with a group of kids his age. He seemed at ease and clowned around with the other guys.

When he made a great play, he looked at me and smiled.

Between games, he sat by me for a few minutes. Our conversations were light and easy. I was happy to see him animated and happy.

At the family meetings, topics ranged from family dynamics to addiction. We stayed at the rehab all day and enjoyed a delicious lunch with Eric and the other families.

On the second night, Eric received permission to eat dinner with us. Since he wasn't allowed to leave the property, he asked us to bring him ribs. We brought them back and ate on a picnic table in the courtyard, enjoying some more easy conversation.

After dinner, we attended an on-site AA meeting.

When we first arrived, Eric's counselor made us tell him he couldn't come home with us. Even with that established, leaving was difficult. Eric wanted to come home.

"You only have two weeks left and you should enjoy them and use them to get better," I said, "You may never again have two weeks to just focus on yourself and nothing else. You should be glad for this opportunity. Use it to heal, so you can come home."

"I know, Mom, but I really want to come home."

I wanted him to come home, too, but I wasn't sure it was such a good idea, even in two weeks. I wanted Eric to go to a halfway house but he didn't want to and his counselor didn't think it'd be necessary.

On one hand, I was happy she was so impressed with his progress. On the other, it didn't seem smart for him to return to his friends and old haunts so soon. I was very apprehensive about Eric's return.

19. Back Home
December 2009–January 2010

Eric came home in early December. My husband and I picked him up at the airport. He looked and sounded great. During our drive home, he couldn't contain himself. He dug through his bag, searching for something.

"Look!" He said, "Look at my thirty-day sobriety medallion from AA and my certificate of completion from the rehab."

His smile lit up his face.

"Eric, that's great," I said, "We're very proud of what you have accomplished during these past thirty days."

"Mom, Dad, staying sober is the most important thing for me, at this point in my life. I feel so good and I am so proud of myself. I will never go back to using drugs again."

I was happy with his enthusiasm but also concerned. We'd learned at the family weekend that the relapse rate for a recovering opiate addict is ninety percent.

Once we got home, Eric immediately wanted to see his friends, which alarmed me.

"Maybe, your friends can come here," I suggested, "Our house can be the sober house, where drinking or drugs will not be allowed."

"Mom, that isn't necessary. Sobriety is the most important thing to me and I won't be tempted to drink or do drugs. Don't worry. I'll be fine."

I hoped his friends would know not to drink or smoke pot in front of Eric. I should have called them before Eric returned home but I hadn't.

Before anything happened, we set down house rules:

He could not go out every night.

He had to meet a curfew, when he did go out.

His friends could not sleep over.

He could not sleep over at friends' houses.

He had to see a psychiatrist on a regular basis.

He had to see a local drug counselor to help him continue with the steps.

He needed to attend Narcotics Anonymous (NA) or Alcoholics Anonymous (AA) meetings at least three to four times a week.

When he resumed working, he needed to pay us $200 a week as rent.

Eric agreed to the rules.

In December, all went well. He stayed home often. When he went out, he abided by the curfew. He found a NA meeting he really liked and even, a sponsor.

He didn't start working right away, which was okay. We felt he needed an adjustment period and wanted him to establish a routine of going to meetings.

The peaceful month made us all feel he was serious about recovery.

When Christmas came along, some of his friends came home for the holiday break. The partying began. At first, he still respected the curfew but, by the middle of January, he came home later and later. The curfew suffered another blow. He began working at the diner again and worked until closing, so he couldn't come home by 1 a.m.

As January continued, he came home at unpredictable times.

The peace in our home was eroding. I sensed my son slipping and could not bear the thought of him falling backwards.

"Never go back," I constantly told him, "Always move forward."

One day toward the end of January, Eric, Jessica, and I were in the kitchen. Eric searched the fridge for something to eat. His anger boiled, then erupted. In his tirade, he admitted he'd smoked pot twice since coming home.

"Eric, no!" I cried out, "You can't do any drugs or drink. If you do, you may become addicted again."

"Mom, I only smoked a joint twice. It's not a big deal."

"Of course, it's a big deal," I shot back, "And you should know better."

Jessica came down hard on him.

"I can't believe that you want to do drugs," she screamed, "I can't believe that you want to be a drug addict. I'm ashamed of you."

Up to that moment, Jessica had been very supportive of her brother's struggle. She had sent him cards with inspirational quotes when he was in rehab. When he returned home, she gave him a compass with a note that read, "Use this when you might begin to lose your way to get back to your family." It was a very clever gift and Eric placed it on his desk where he saw it, when he woke up each morning.

Her severe reaction set him off.

"What the fuck do I care what you think?" he yelled, "I can do drugs if I want to and if I do, it doesn't mean that I will become addicted again."

"Eric, of course, you'll become addicted again," I said, "You know that. You can't possibly think that you can do drugs without becoming addicted."

"What the fuck? Just leave me alone. I can do what I want," he screamed, quickly leaving the kitchen.

Once things calmed down, I talked to each of them alone and tried to smooth things over. I worried about how the exchange would affect their relationship.

I reminded Eric that he cannot smoke pot, drink, or take any type of drug. I reminded him of all the things he learned in rehab. I was *very* upset. What if he'd done more than smoke pot twice? What if he became addicted again? I didn't know if I could handle that.

By the end of January, Eric pleaded with me to let him move in with a friend who lived forty-five minutes away.

"You can afford the rent there and car insurance and food on a waiter's salary?" I asked, "I don't think so."

"I can pay my portion of the rent," he said, "Besides, if I don't move away from this town, I'm going to use again. There's too much temptation here."

His friend called to assure me he and his brother wanted to help Eric stay away from drugs. I relented. Eric agreed to come home for dinner every Thursday night. He called me often.

"It's working out, Mom," he said, "One of my friends is always with me."

One evening, he came home unexpectedly, saying he missed us. I wasn't sure if I believed him. My gut told me he was tired of his friends' twenty-four-hour surveillance and came home to buy drugs or find a way to do them.

We had dinner. He stayed until eight o'clock. Although, he didn't leave my sight for more than a few minutes at a time, I still felt uneasy and suspicious about why he came home.

About a week later, Mike, one of his roommates, called me.

"Mrs. Burns, I think he's using again," he said, "I know when he's high."

Like me, Mike didn't know what to do.

"What you and your brother are doing is difficult and I appreciate your concern for Eric," I said.

"We'll keep steering him away from drugs," he said, "But I don't know if we'll be able to do it."

Mike called a few days later to say that Eric was making mistakes at work and that he was certain Eric was using.

"What do I do?" he asked.

"We've got to get him into detox," I said.

I checked with my insurance company and found a hospital close to where Eric lived. Mike said he'd bring Eric there that very day.

Later that afternoon, the phone rang. It was Eric. He slurred his words.

"Where are you?" I asked, panicked.

"I'm driving, Mom. I can't find the hospital. Where is the hospital? Can you give me directions?"

"Where is Mike?" I asked, panic rising in my throat.

"Oh, he had a doctor's appointment. He's going to meet me at the hospital. Do you know where the hospital is?"

"Get off the road!" I yelled, "You shouldn't be driving when you're high. Get off the road!"

"Mom, I'm fine. I just need to find the hospital."

"No, you are not fine! You could have an accident and possibly kill yourself or someone else. Get off the road *now* and call Mike. He can pick you up after his appointment."

I kept pleading with him. Somehow, he arrived safely at the hospital. Mike called me later.

"I'm sorry, Mrs. Burns, for not cancelling my appointment but I really thought Eric wanted to get better. I really thought he would go straight to the hospital. I never thought he would get high first."

I was relieved, upset, and grateful, all at the same time.

Eric was admitted to the detox unit, which gave him drugs to lessen his withdrawal pain but he was still in some pain. Secretly, I was glad. If the experience was painful, maybe he'd remember it and never put himself through it again.

I talked to him every day. He sounded miserable and lost. On the third day, I called his counselor. On the fourth day, Eric was to be released.

"Will Eric be expected to get outpatient counseling after he is released?" I asked. "Will he be given a list of NA or AA meetings in the area? Will there be any follow-up once he's released?"

His counselor was sympathetic.

"We can give him a list of NA and AA meetings in the area," he said, "But no, he won't get any follow-up or outpatient counseling."

"But why have him detox if no one is going to follow up with him and help him continue to stay away from drugs?"

"There's a chance Eric may go back to using drugs after he leaves," he said, "But he also might be able to stay on the road to recovery, if he attends meetings."

"But I don't understand. No one is going to help him? It doesn't make sense to have him detox and then not help him stay drug free."

"You have to understand," he said, "Sometimes, even a drug addict needs a break from doing drugs."

I was stunned. *What does that mean? Was four days in detox just to give my son a break from doing drugs? Was it expected he'd use the second he was released?* I'd thought detox was the first step toward becoming drug free. Did anybody care?

"I will speak with Eric to see if he's willing to go to another rehab," he said, "I know a place in Florida, where people have had positive results."

I breathed a sigh of relief. He *was* willing to get involved. He called me back within a half hour.

"I just spoke to Eric and he has agreed to go to another inpatient rehab," he said.

I was thrilled. The counselor gave me a contact name and I made arrangements for Eric to arrive at the rehab the following day. I also booked him a flight. Then, I called back the counselor to let him know.

"You need to bring Eric directly from the hospital to the airport tomorrow," he said, "Do *not* let him go home. He will only go home to get high. If you let him go home, you may never get him to the airport."

I talked to Mike, who agreed to pick Eric up the next day and drive him to the airport.

"Don't give Eric his car keys," I told Mike. "Remember, take him *directly* to the airport."

"I understand, Mrs. Burns."

Eric was to be discharged from the hospital on a Sunday. I called him at 10 a.m. to tell him of the arrangements.

"Mike will be there in a little while," I told him, "Once you're discharged, he'll bring you to the airport. I booked you on a 5:30 flight. We'll meet you at the airport. I'll bring a packed bag, so you'll have what you need for rehab."

He was incensed.

"What do you mean I have to go right to the airport?!" he said, "Why can't I go home first? I don't want to go right to Florida. I want to go home first."

"You can't come home first. The rehab in Florida is expecting you tonight. We'll meet you at the airport, so you can see us and say good bye."

He begged.

"Please, Mom, *please,* I just want to go home for one night. I just want to sleep in my bed for one night and spend some time with you guys. I can go to Florida on Monday. *Please* let me come home for just one night. *Please...*"

For as much as I wanted to believe him, I didn't. He wanted to come home to get high because he knew where to get drugs here. I didn't need to worry about him sneaking out of the house to get high. I didn't need to fight with him the next day to get him to the airport. I just needed him on the plane.

"I *won't* go to Florida, if you don't let me go home first," he screamed, "*Please* let me go home for one night. *P-l-e-a-s-e.*"

"You *cannot* come home," I yelled back. "You *must* go right to the airport."

"Mike's here," he said. He hung up the phone.

An hour later, Mike called.

"Eric's been discharged," he said. "I want to take him to the airport now to meet you guys but he won't get into my car and he is demanding that I give him his car keys. What should I do?"

"Do *not* give him his car keys."

"But he won't get into my car. So, what should I do?"

"Do *not* give him his keys. He is *not* allowed to have his car back. If he won't go to the airport, he'll have to sleep on the street tonight. You *cannot* let him stay at your place tonight."

Mike hesitated.

"I don't know if I can do that."

"You have to. We must stand together and be tough. He needs help and he needs to go to Florida. You *cannot* give him his keys. He *cannot* come home and he *cannot* stay at your apartment, if he refuses to go to the rehab."

Again, he hesitated.

"But, Mrs. Burns, I really don't know if I can do that. I'll call you back."

I immediately called Eric's counselor from the hospital.

"Eric is refusing to go to the airport," I said, "He's saying he just wants to go home first to spend the night with us. What should I do? Should I let him come home?"

"No!" he exclaimed. "If you let him go home, there is a good chance you won't be able to get him to the airport tomorrow. I'll call him and see if I can talk some sense into him."

I sat at my kitchen table and cried. *What if we don't get him to the airport? What would happen to him? How was I supposed to go on, knowing he was on the street because of me? How did we get here?*

I just wanted him to get well. Why didn't *he* want to get well? I said a prayer.

"Dear Lord, please help Eric make the right decision. Please make him realize he needs help and he needs to get on that plane. *Please* get him on that plane."

I busied myself to keep my mind occupied. I washed dishes, threw in a load of laundry, put away clean clothes, and swept the kitchen floor. Even so, the thought of my son homeless haunted me. *He's only twenty.*

Suddenly the phone rang, startling me out of my thoughts. I quickly picked it up and glanced at the kitchen clock; one o'clock. It was Mike.

"I'm taking Eric to the airport now."

"Okay. Does he want us to meet him there?"

"I don't know. He's not talking to me right now. I'll call you back."

Almost immediately, the phone rang again. It was Eric, sounding subdued.

"Aren't you going to come to the airport?"

"We will, if you want us to."

"Yeah, I want to see everyone before I leave."

I told my husband that Eric was on his way to the airport and that we needed to leave to see him off.

"Let's go," he said, "Jessica, Matthew, get in the car."

Both of them were still upset and angry with their brother. Jessica rebelled.

"I don't need to go to the airport. Why should I want to see Eric off?" she said, "If he wants to be a drug addict, that's his problem. I don't need to see him."

Matthew rebelled, too.

"I don't really want to go to the airport, either," he said, "Why do we have to go?"

Like everyone else, they didn't understand why Eric wanted to destroy himself.

Both my husband and I insisted that they see their brother off. We both felt it was important that Eric saw we all still supported him. I grabbed the packed suitcase.

The ride to Newark was quiet. Jessica and Matthew were in the back seat, eyes closed, listening to their iPods. I glanced at my husband, intent on driving. How calm they seemed. My mind raced with thoughts about Eric and his addiction. *What if he failed in Florida and couldn't overcome his addiction? If he ends up living on the street, at least, he'll be in Florida where it's warm.* What a horrible thought. *Dear Lord, please help my son get better, please.*

We parked and walked across the street into the terminal, immediately spotting Eric and Mike near the entrance. Eric hugged each of us. He'd lost weight in the past four days. His clothes looked looser, his face thinner.

Mike handed Eric's car keys to my husband.

"Thank you for getting him here," I said.

I hugged Mike. He left.

Eric immediately opened the suitcase I'd packed and added things he'd brought to the hospital. He quickly closed it and we all went to the counter and checked it. Before Eric went through security, we found a place to eat and talk as a family. The harsh lights of the crowded and noisy food court blinded me, intensifying the headache I'd had since morning. *This is not a good place for a serious family discussion.* No other options were available, though, so we bought meals and sat down.

The tension among us was thick. Eric, Jessica, and Matthew didn't speak to each other.

Eric ate his burrito with gusto. Sweat beaded on his forehead. Occasionally, he wiped it away with a napkin. *Is he still detoxing?* I wasn't sure.

While we ate, my husband and I told Eric that we loved him and that we wanted to see him well. We also reminded him that if he wanted to live at home, he had to be drug free.

"You don't need to do this for us," I said, "You need to do it for yourself. You have a lot to live for."

He quietly listened and nodded, as he ate.

"I know, I know," he said.

After the meal, we walked him to the security line and hugged him one last time. I cried.

"*Please* get better, Eric," I said, "*Please.*"

The line was short. We watched him. Once he was through, I stood, frozen, unable to take my eyes off him, as he walked toward the gate ever farther away. I watched until he was out of sight and wondered if I'd ever see him again.

20. Beautiful Boy
March 2010

Eric arrived in Florida safely but called a couple of nights later in a panic.

"Mom, this place is horrible. They won't let me use the phone and they don't give me enough food to eat," he said, "It's not like Texas. The people there knew what they were doing. At this rehab, the people don't know what they're doing. The patients fight and they basically run their own meetings. They're not teaching me anything. A month here will be a waste of time. If I have to be in a rehab, I want to go back to Texas."

He barely caught his breath and went on.

"I jumped over the fence that surrounds the rehab," he said, "I'm calling from the convenience store down the street."

Panic shot through my body.

"What do you mean you jumped the fence? I'm going to call the people down there and talk to someone."

I was shocked he could leave the facility so easily.

"No, Mom, don't call anyone," he said, "Just let me come home. I don't need to be here."

"Go back to the rehab!" I screamed at him and slammed the phone down.

I immediately called our contact at the rehab, who called some staffers. In a few minutes, my contact called back.

"Eric has returned," he said.

But I was still upset. Again, I'd sent my son to a place for help, sight unseen. Again, he told me I'd made a mistake. And, this time, he easily escaped without anyone's knowledge.

I couldn't sleep that night. The next day, I went to work thinking I could somehow make it through the day, but I couldn't hold back the tears. As soon as a colleague greeted me, I cried.

Before the students arrived for a test, I composed myself. I handed out the testing material, keeping my head low, and letting the other teacher give the directions. Shortly, the test was under way.

"Go take a break," my colleague told me.

I met another teacher in the hallway, who saw I was upset. We talked. The principal saw me, too. Up to that point, I'd worked very hard to keep my personal problems separate from my work but that was no longer possible. I was an emotional mess. I could hardly talk to my principal through my tears.

I never returned to the testing room. The principal sent me home but insisted I talk to the school's drug counselor first.

The counselor and I spoke for a half hour.

"The journey of addiction and recovery for Eric and your family has just begun," she explained, "Eric is still young and there's a good chance he won't be willing or able to give up his drug-using ways, at this point, in his life."

This journey would get even longer? I was horrified.

Talking to someone who understood addiction felt good but I left troubled. *What was still to come?*

As soon as I walked into my house, I called the rehab's director for some answers.

"Why was my son able to escape so easily? Isn't there staff at night watching the patients? Are you really going to help Eric?"

She instantly put me at ease. At that moment, she said, Eric's counselor was talking to him about his escape.

"We don't allow people to call during their first week at the rehab," the director said, "We feel they need a week to settle in. Don't worry. Eric is in good hands. I love all the kids that come here."

"When they arrive, they think they can take drugs forever and it's difficult to get them to think otherwise, especially the first week," she added, "I'll make it my personal business to talk to Eric every day, even for just a few minutes. Call me any time to check on his progress."

She promised that Eric's counselor and the director of counseling would call me.

After speaking to both, I realized Eric's arrival and escape had thrown the place into crisis mode.

"We've talked to him most of the morning," the director of counseling said, "Eric is not receptive to being in rehab, at this point. He doesn't want to be here. He's angry you didn't allow him to go home before going to the airport."

After a very tense meeting, Eric's counselor offered him the seventy-eight cents he had when he arrived at the rehab.

"Go ahead," he told Eric, "You can leave."

At that point, Eric broke down. Seventy-eight cents allowed him to call us but we would not buy him a plane ticket. He knew he couldn't come home a drug addict. He knew he had nowhere to go.

Eric was trapped. His tears signaled resignation. He had one choice; to get better.

After the first week, Eric was allowed to call twice a week.

The first call was very tense.

"Please, Mom, please let me come home."

"You cannot come home unless you get better. You need to stay at the rehab, so you can get better."

"Mom, you don't understand. I need to come home because that's where I can get heroin."

I couldn't believe what he'd just said.

"I cannot condone your drug use. If you insist on using drugs, you will have to stay in Florida far away from home because I cannot and will not watch you kill yourself. Drug addiction is just slow suicide. If you don't stop using, you will eventually end up dead."

"I won't kill myself, Mom. I know what I'm doing."

Again, I couldn't believe what came out of his mouth.

"Most drug addicts who die from an overdose don't wake up and say, "I think I'll overdose today." Overdosing is usually accidental."

"I'm not going to overdose, Mom. I need to come home, Mom. Really, I do."

He continued pleading until his phone time was up. He had to get off and allow other patients a chance to use the phone.

"I'll call back later," he said.

"I love you," I said, "And I want you back healthy and drug-free."

After we finished our talk, I understood how much the drug controlled him. I wasn't sure talk therapy was enough for him.

A more subdued Eric called back a couple of hours later.

"Mom, I'm going to do my best to get better," he said, "I shouldn't expect you to be okay with me using drugs. Really, I'm going to try to get better."

"I'm glad to hear that," I said, "Since we talked earlier, I've been thinking you need more than talk therapy to get better. The drugs have more of a hold on your brain this time. I'm going to call the rehab's doctor tomorrow to see if he can give you medicine."

"That's probably a good idea."

"Eric, we just want you to get better," I reminded him.

"I know, Mom, I know."

I don't know how much heroin Eric used before he went into detox but it had to be a relatively large amount, judging by the difficulty he had accepting he could no longer use. We hadn't gone through this in the first rehab. The opiates had tighter grip on him this time.

His body had become accustomed to drugs and he couldn't have them. He was in pain. Eric was talking through a lot of pain. He could only worry about this physical pain and how drugs could alleviate it. He couldn't see beyond it. He certainly couldn't see how his choices affected his family.

When he went to Texas, I felt Eric had made a mistake. Like many kids his age, he partied too much and got 'caught' because of a possible genetic predisposition to addiction.

After that phone conversation, I knew he was a hard-core addict. The drugs wanted my son and it seemed they wouldn't leave him alone. The thought scared me.

I couldn't sleep. In my mind, I replayed Eric's words, "Mom, you don't understand. I need to come home because that's where I can get heroin."

What if the drugs had already won the battle for my son? I got up at three-thirty in the morning and sat in the dark family room for forty-five minutes.

Deciding I needed to write a letter, I walked to the kitchen, turned on the light, found a piece of lined paper, and wrote:

Dear Eric,

It is 4:15 in the morning and I can't get you out of my mind. I've been up since 3:30 and I am too sad to fall back to sleep or think of anything but you and the situation that you are in. When I was flying to Texas, I read a book called *Beautiful Boy*. It is a story written by the father of a drug addict about his journey through addiction with his son. Throughout the book, he shares painful memories of how he watches his son destroy himself and how he can't seem to help him. It horrifies me to think that I am, now, that man. I now share some of his pain and I have the same questions he has.

- Where is my beautiful boy?
- Why is he choosing drugs over life?
- How can I help him?
- Why does he have such low self-esteem?
- Why does he want to destroy himself?
- What could I have done differently?
- What can I do to help my beautiful boy?
- Where is my beautiful boy?

I'm not saying that you're not beautiful; in fact, you are and will always be beautiful to me. The question is, why are you trying to destroy the beautiful boy named Eric Burns? Please, Eric, stop destroying yourself and allow your beautiful self to come to the surface.

I'm now reading another book called *A Million Little Pieces*. This book is written by a recovering drug addict. He was told at the age of twenty-three that he had done so much damage to his body that if he drank or did drugs again, he would be dead in a matter of days. Not being of sound mind, he initially decides that he is going to run away from the rehab, get high/drunk one *last* time, and die. He feels he has caused others so much pain that he is not worthy. He thinks nobody will miss him. Well, some things happen to him, some people show care and concern for him and he changes his mind. He learns that not only does his family and friends, whom he believed wrote him off, still care about him but so do complete strangers at the rehab.

I hope, Eric, that you understand how much your family and friends care about you. We are all very worried and we can't believe that you might actually not want to get better.

The book also takes readers through the detox process. This ex-addict very clearly relays how difficult it is to go through. He talks about how powerful the urge for drugs is, how physically painful it can be, and the mental anguish it causes. I know I can't feel the mental and physical pain you are going through but I certainly have a clearer picture after reading his struggle. I can only pray that you can be strong enough to get through this painful process and choose to fight the urge to get high. If you fight this urge, then you are choosing life, you are choosing to live. If you give into it, you are choosing death. *Please* choose life.

Eric, I constantly pray and ask God to help you, to make his presence known to you. I know that he is with you. Please let him into your heart and allow the healing process to begin. Your counselor, this time around, may not be an ex-addict but she doesn't have to be to help you. She only needs to help you get inside your head and heart, so you can find out what causes you so much pain. Please let her help you. Please talk about things that might be painful to you. Once you get to this pain, the healing process can begin.

I love you, Eric, and want to see you well. Please call and let us know how you are doing.

Love,
Mom xxoo

And, then, I quickly scribbled the following poem.

Where is my beautiful boy?
Where did he go?
It seems like only yesterday that
he was cooking me a pretend dinner,
hitting home runs,
and being Tommy, the Power Ranger,
with me as Kimberly.
Only yesterday that he was riding his bike,
building sandcastles at the lake,
and body surfing in the ocean
Where is my beautiful boy?
I want him back
I want to play games with him again,
go swimming and to the ocean with him again
Where is my beautiful boy?
Where did he go?
I want him back

The poem, like the letter, dripped with my pain. Eric had to hear it. He had to understand the pain his addiction caused me. I mailed the letter on my way to work.

A few days later, Eric called, "Hi, Mom."

His voice was so low, I could hardly hear him.

"Is everything okay?"

"I got your letter today. I cried like a baby while I was reading it. Actually, I probably cried for about an hour. I couldn't stop crying. The poem you wrote at the end made me cry even more. I didn't realize how hard this is for you and everyone else in the family. I'm going to get better, Mom. I am. I'm going to get better for you."

After the call, I felt a great weight lift off my shoulders. I even smiled.

Maybe, just maybe, he would get better.

21. Florida
Spring 2010

By the end of the first week, Eric had settled down. Then, the rehab called to say our insurance company would cover only two weeks of treatment. I was floored. *How do they expect him to get better in only two weeks?*

"There's no way he's leaving in only two weeks," I said.

"We'll try to get the insurance company to change their minds."

Later that day, they called back: the insurance company would pay for three weeks and the rehab would give Eric a fourth week on scholarship.

For the remainder of his time, Eric did extremely well. His change in attitude impressed his counselors. By the end of the third week, we talked about what he'd do after rehab. My husband and I didn't want him to come home right away. Returning to the same environment, same friends, and same job, the same triggers, would tempt him to use.

We all decided Eric should live in a halfway house with oversight that would drug-test him regularly. His counselor recommended a place. I made the arrangements. I hoped Eric would stay in Florida six months to a year.

The Thursday before Easter, I picked him up at the airport for a short visit. I entered the terminal just as he picked his luggage off the carousel. When he saw me, he flashed a big smile and gave me one of his big bear hugs. He looked great and sounded very positive as we talked on the way home.

Though ecstatic to have him home for the weekend, I also was nervous he'd want to go out with his friends. We'd hidden all the extra car keys and directed Jessica and Matthew not to leave their keys anywhere Eric could easily find them.

During the entire weekend, Eric never asked to use the car. Never once did he ask to see his friends. He seemed very content to spend time with his family. He went shopping Saturday afternoon with Jessica; I was happy to see them reconnect. Later in the day, he and Matthew played video games. We also dyed Easter eggs and had an Easter egg hunt on Sunday morning. I couldn't believe the three of them still wanted me to hide Easter eggs but I thought, *Why not?*

They searched the downstairs rooms while goofing around and fighting over their finds. Easter Sunday afternoon, we went to my sister's house for dinner. The weekend passed peacefully.

I drove Eric to the airport Monday, so he could return to Florida. After we checked his bags, we had breakfast and talked.

"Thanks for such a great weekend. I was great to have you home," I said, "I was nervous you would demand to use the car and want to see your friends and that we would end up fighting."

"Mom, I really just wanted to come home and spend time with the family. Seeing my friends wasn't why I wanted to come home."

Hearing his family was becoming more important to him made me smile.

"Mom, I know that I can't come home yet. When I went shopping with Jessica the other day, I didn't feel comfortable near certain areas; places near where I used to buy drugs. These places reminded me of drugs too much. I can't come home at this point, Mom. I really can't."

Maybe he was beginning to understand addiction and realizing he needed to let his brain heal. I felt good about sending him to a halfway house; a logical next step. He left in a very positive state of mind.

Late that afternoon, Eric called to tell me he'd arrived safely in Florida. *Still sounding positive*. I breathed a sigh of relief.

But it didn't take long for Eric's positive state of mind to change. The next day he called again.

"Mom, this place is disgusting. It's filthy and there are drugs everywhere. It's also in a really bad area and the cops are always being called."

I didn't know what to think. I'd received desperate phone calls from each rehab. *Are things really that bad or is he just pulling on my heartstrings because he wants to come home?*

I tried to sound upbeat.

"Eric, it might not be the nicest place but there's supposed to be a bus service, so you can get to the business area. Find out about that service and try and look for a job," I advised, "Once you get a job, you may be able to move to your own place. Also, there are staff people, who are supposed to help you. Go to the office and ask them for help. Maybe they can give you some cleaning supplies, so you can clean the apartment. That might make you feel more comfortable."

"Mom, the other kids here say that there isn't a bus service. Whoever told you that, lied to you. The stores are a half-mile away and it's too hot to walk to them. By the time I walk to the stores, I'd be so sweaty and smelly, I couldn't go into a business and ask for a job. I'd look gross. This place is disgusting, Mom, and I don't want to stay here."

"What about the people in the office? Have you spoken to them? Can they help you?"

"No, Mom, they don't care. They aren't going to do anything to help me."

Again, I wasn't sure whether to believe him. I encouraged him to ask his friend in the area to bring him to the local department store.

"Use the gift card I gave you to buy cleaning supplies and clean the apartment, so it feels more like home."

"I shouldn't have to clean up such a disgusting mess, especially since I didn't make it," he said, "Mom, it's gross. There are dead cockroaches in the kitchen."

Again, I'd sent my son more than a thousand miles away to a recommended place, thinking he'd get help and direction to stay in recovery. Yet, his complaints continued.

"One of my roommates is from the rehab and he's an asshole," Eric told me, "I really don't like him. No one cleans up and I don't think that I should clean up after them."

I didn't like what I heard but I didn't know what to do. I called my contact at the halfway house.

"My son needs some direction," I told her, "Help him, please."

She said she would.

Eric said she never did. It seemed that Eric had to figure things out by himself.

I'd made two doctor's appointments for Eric shortly after his arrival; one with a hepatologist for his Hepatitis B, the other with a psychiatrist. I wanted Eric to stay on Naltroxene to curb his need for drugs. Finding a psychiatrist certified to prescribe it had been a challenge but I succeeded.

Eric walked to the psychiatrist's office in the extreme heat. The appointment did not go well. He called me afterward.

"Mom, I don't like the psychiatrist. He's just a fast talker. First of all, he drug-tested me. Was he supposed to do that? He also gave me another shot of Naltroxene without asking me if I wanted it."

"He actually told me I had a high chance of relapse. Why would he tell me that? Shouldn't he be encouraging me? What a stupid thing for him to say. I don't like him, Mom, and I think he just wants to make money and that he really doesn't care about whether I get better or not. I'm *not* going back to him."

I was glad Eric got the shot but unhappy about the appointment. The doctor called me later that evening, expressing worry that Eric would relapse and trying to sell me his program, which included small group, large group, and individual therapy sessions for one month.

"With that type of intervention, Eric will have a much better chance at recovery," he said, "The cost is only six thousand dollars for the month."

I listened closely because I, too, was worried about relapse but he lost me when he told me his program would *only* cost six thousand dollars. I also felt he was a fast talker. I didn't want to deal with him, either.

When Eric called the next day, I was at school. He sounded extremely depressed. I could hardly hear him. Finally, I made out what he was saying.

"Mom, I failed the last drug test I was given. I took a pill yesterday because I thought that it would kill me. I can't stand being here. I'm so depressed and just want to die. I really thought taking this pill would kill me because you're not supposed to be able to do drugs with Naltroxene in your system."

I couldn't believe my ears.

How did my son, who was so positive just two weeks earlier, become suicidal? I panicked. I was more than a thousand miles away. I told him to call his friend down the street and ask to stay with him a few days. In the meantime, we'd come up with a plan.

"No, Mom, I can't do that. I'm so ashamed of what I've done."

I told him to stay put.

"I'll call you right back."

I immediately called my husband, who happened to be in Florida on business.

"Cancel your dinner appointment," I said, "Go see Eric. We need to know if the halfway house is really as bad as he says."

He agreed to go.

I, then, called the halfway house and left a very nasty message. I was angry. I blamed them for Eric's quick decline.

"If anything happens to him, I'll sue you," I said.

They never returned my call.

By the time my husband arrived that evening, Eric had been retested and passed. That meant he got a second chance; he could stay at the halfway house. My husband stayed with him for an hour and called me, saying the apartment, with a little cleaning, could be made respectable.

"The halfway house is part of a compound," he explained, "It houses recovering drug addicts and other people."

I was confused. *Is that legal? A halfway house is supposed to be a controlled environment. How can this environment be controlled, if anybody can live there?*

I wasn't happy with my husband's report but heartened they gave Eric a second chance; albeit, on one-month probation. He'd be drug tested more often and get an earlier-than-usual curfew. He was also required to do community service at the halfway house. I approved the arrangement because it required the staff to give Eric extra attention.

My husband suggested I take off from work and visit Eric in Florida, so I made arrangements. Not right away, though. I gave Eric time to find another halfway house. *If the place he's living is that bad*, I thought, *maybe we should move him.*

I called a few places in the area and got basic information I relayed to Eric, suggesting he visit them if he could find someone to drive him.

"We can move you into one when I visit," I said, "If that's what you want."

The week before my visit, Eric's phone calls become more positive. He'd made friends, which helped his mood.

I arrived in West Palm Beach late Friday morning and drove to the halfway house. I was immediately unhappy with what I saw. From the outside, the compound, with small, attached units painted a light yellow, didn't look bad. Some effort had gone into landscaping.

When I entered Eric's apartment, though, my heart broke. He stood in the dining room area and stared at the floor, unable to look at me. He didn't give me one of his great big bear hugs. He said nothing. I hugged him.

"I'm glad to see you," I said.

I instantly saw why he'd become so depressed. The living room couches were so matted down with filth, I didn't want to sit on them. The space between the glass top and wood of the coffee table was filled with years' worth of dirt. The bathrooms should have been gutted. The porcelain that coated the tubs had been so worn away, they both appeared gray.

The kitchen was the worst. The cabinets were covered with sticky grime. I understood why Eric refused to cook in it. He only cooked in the apartment next door, which was a lot cleaner. His place was every bit as disgusting as he said it was.

We immediately left the premises and went to lunch. Once out of the halfway house, his demeanor brightened and we talked easily.

"Do you want to move to another halfway house?" I asked, "If you do, I can move you while I'm down here."

"I don't know, Mom. Even though this place is gross, I've made some friends and I don't know if I want to go to a place where I won't know anyone."

"I realize that might be hard for you but if we can find a different place that is cleaner and that will give you more help and support, it might be good for you."

"My friend Rob isn't really happy, either, but his father just paid the next month's rent, so he won't be able to move out for another month."

"Talk to Rob and see if he wants to move to another place. If he does, you'll have a month to find one you both like."

After lunch, we bought groceries and cleaning supplies at a local store. When we returned to the apartment, we tackled the kitchen cabinets; wiping down the shelves and cabinet doors, until the sticky crude came off.

By the time we finished, we both felt the kitchen could actually be used for cooking and storing food.

I told the woman, who worked in the office, that my husband and I owned apartment buildings in a city near where we live.

"We would *never* rent our apartments in such deplorable conditions," I said, "Plus, only people in recovery should be allowed to live here. I saw one of my son's neighbors, who's not part of the halfway house smoking pot outside, right next to the entrance to my son's apartment."

"Whenever we see him smoking, we call the police," she assured me.

I didn't believe her and vowed to have the place shut down after Eric returned home or moved somewhere else.

Eric and I spent the afternoon, at my hotel on the beach and took a couple of nice, long walks. As the day progressed, Eric became much more positive. We also discussed moving him closer to home. I'd explored a place in Connecticut about two hours from our house that referred to itself as 'transitional housing.'

The program was divided into three phases.

The first was, somewhat, like rehab; offering group and individual therapy. Clients were expected to do chores and go to the gym. Staffers transported them to AA or NA meetings. They also met with clients in later phases of the program.

The second phase allowed clients some free time to hunt for a job or explore going back to school. They learned resume writing and interview skills.

In the third phase, they lived independently in a halfway house arrangement with oversight.

Eric read the booklet I'd brought but felt the arrangement might be too constricting, even a step backwards in terms of his independence. Though I felt the program would be good for him, he needed to make the decision on where to go. Otherwise, he might not commit to it.

I wanted Eric to stay with me at my hotel, so he could have a mini-vacation but he couldn't. Since he was on probation, he was not allowed off the halfway house premises overnight.

We enjoyed each other all day Saturday. I offered to visit other halfway houses with him and to move him but he wasn't interested. Instead, he looked for job openings on the Internet. I brought him to one place to put in an application. That evening, we went to dinner with his friend Rob in downtown Delray Beach.

On Sunday morning, I picked him up for a late breakfast. Although his demeanor had become much more positive since I arrived, he was upset when I picked him up. Deep down, I knew he wanted to come home with me. I would have loved that, but it was still too soon.

At times, he looked as if he'd cry. I kept the conversation light, told him we all loved him, and that before he came home, he needed to figure out his next step in life. School? Or a type of business? If so, what schooling or training did that field require? He listened quietly.

As a parent, I always wanted to take care of my children but I realized I might not be able to care for Eric, especially if he returned home prematurely. The last thing I wanted was for him to use drugs again.

I dropped him off at the halfway house and, with a heavy heart, headed to the airport. I couldn't be sure leaving him in Florida was the right thing to do.

As May progressed, Eric and I talked many times; sometimes, pleasantly and sometimes, not. He was getting depressed again. Without transportation, he still didn't have a job. Although he lived three-tenths of a mile from the main road, he couldn't walk. The heat was too intense. He didn't tolerate heat well. Would he begin to use?

Two weeks after I returned from my Florida visit, I told my husband Eric should come home. I felt the halfway house was not beneficial to his recovery. My husband agreed that Eric could come home.

When I told Eric, his reply was guarded.

"I don't know, Mom," he said, "I'm not sure that's a good idea. Let me think about it."

I was surprised but also saw his response as a good sign. After pondering one day, he decided to stay in Florida. After that, our conversations became more positive.

In New Jersey, we planned for Matthew's High School graduation in June. We told Eric he could come home for the celebration and buy a car, while he was in New Jersey. He still had the bank account containing his rent money. If he returned to Florida with a car, we hoped he'd find a job.

"Think about what type of car you want," I said, giving him something to look forward to.

Eric visited in June, as planned, and it was nice to have him home. He helped me cook for the graduation party. Everyone, who tasted his chicken dish, loved it. He saw some of his old friends but abided by his curfew.

He and his father went car shopping for a Nissan Altima. Registration and inspection took a week. On the Fourth of July, Eric and I headed south to Florida. We talked a lot during the two-day road trip. He looked forward to seeing his friends at the halfway house. He also knew that, with a car, he'd be able to find a job. I hoped the independence it gave him would enable him to move forward with his life.

I spent two days with him. We went to dinner Monday with two of his friends. On Tuesday, I bought him groceries and we had lunch. Then, I filled up his gas tank, rented a car, and said goodbye.

"I love you, Eric," I said, "You've got a car, so find work. Now, you have no excuse."

He assured me he would. He was tired of doing nothing and wanted to help pay the bills. The halfway house had cost us six hundred dollars a month. Between that, the airline tickets, hotel rooms, and rental cars, we'd had a very expensive few months.

22. Never Look Back
August 2010

Three weeks after returning to Florida, Eric called one night.

"I can't live here anymore. If I stay, I'll be tempted to begin using drugs again. I hate the hot Florida heat and I can't find a job. Mom, I hate it here," he said, "I want to come home. I'll find a job and then look into culinary school. Staying here is not helping me anymore. I'm just wasting my time."

Both my husband and I agreed with him. We sent him money for gas and a hotel room. He and his friend, Rob, who is from upstate New York, drove north and arrived at our house at 1:15 a.m. August 1, 2010. Eric woke me up and kissed me.

"Love you, Mom," he said.

Rob stayed a few days because his parents were on vacation. Once they returned, Eric drove him home.

At that point, I told Eric he needed to get serious about job hunting. We also talked about making appointments to visit two culinary schools he liked. I was hopeful but also worried. My job was to guide and help him but I couldn't make his decisions.

I'm the kind of person who does what needs to be done. Eric was the kind of person who does what's required, eventually. In the weeks and months ahead, we'd no doubt butt heads and argue but, hopefully, he'd understand I bothered him to do things because I wanted him to reach any goals he set for himself.

"Never look backward," I reminded him, "Only look forward. Forgive yourself and move on."

He'd come home expecting to kick his drug addiction, but, again, he could not seem to do it. He hung out with his old friends, who still partied. Like a lot of addicts, he started believing he could drink occasionally and then smoke pot. We'd begun to suspect he was using again. We recognized the signs, including disappearing for long periods of time for no apparent reason. I again searched the house looking for evidence but found nothing.

After a brief search, Eric hadn't found a job. His boss at the diner was nice enough to rehire him, so Eric returned to work there. I didn't like the idea from the start and encouraged him to keep looking for a different job, one far away from his familiar turf and triggers. The whole situation made me queasy.

Late one evening in mid-October, a friend from the diner drove Eric home. He'd gone to work high and his boss asked him to leave. Instead of just coming home, he became depressed and drove to his dealer. He'd had enough sense to drive back to the diner and ask someone for a lift home but I wasn't happy with the situation that we faced, again.

His friend walked him into the house. We thanked him.

The moment he was out the door, I turned to Eric.

"You have to detox," I said, "You can't stay home in this condition."

He agreed. We decided I'd drive him to the hospital and my husband would retrieve Eric's car at the diner. The moment my husband was out the door, Eric turned to me.

"Mom, I'm not going to the hospital."

"You either go to the hospital, Eric, or you have to leave the house. You can't live in this house, when you're using drugs."

"That's okay. One of my friends will pick me up. I'm not going to the hospital."

He wanted to detox at a friend's house. I didn't argue. I was tired of arguing. I let him call a friend and leave.

He detoxed on his own, couch surfing from one friend's house to the next. He kept in touch and asked me to get Suboxone from his psychiatrist.

"By the time I reach the doctor and the pharmacist gets the drug, your three to four days of pain and agony will be over," I told him.

He suffered through the detox on his own. I knew how painful and potentially dangerous detox was supposed to be but I was also angry. Part of me hoped that if he suffered enough, he'd stop doing this to himself.

After about a week, he returned home.

"Mom, I am done with drugs," he said, "I am never going through that again."

I wanted to believe him. I truly did.

In a month, he landed a new job at a group home working with developmentally disabled adults. He quickly fell in love with it. His boss gave him rave reviews. I loved seeing him excited about work and getting so much satisfaction from what he did. His spirits always rose, when he talked about his clients. Some Sundays, after church, I met Eric at a local coffee shop where he introduced me to some of them.

Life was good for a couple of months. Then, things changed for the worse.

One Saturday, my husband asked Eric to work with him in the apartments we own. Eric worked all day and came home tired. Even so, he went out.

"I'm going to a friend's house," he told us.

He went to see his dealer.

At 10:30 that night, the police called. The inevitable had happened. Eric was stopped and charged with a DUI. He'd have to stand in front of a judge and face the music.

When I picked him up, I was livid. *What happened?* I was so sure he hadn't been using drugs. I'd had him drug-tested twice in the last three months. He'd passed both tests. He had a job he loved. Life was going well. *Why? Why?*

When I entered the police station, Eric stood, relaxed, conversing with the officer. I signed the papers for his release.

"He's really a nice kid," the officer said.

"I know," I replied, "He just makes bad choices."

During our drive home, I asked Eric the question burning in my mind.

"What happened? I thought you weren't using drugs," I said, "I thought you did it this time and weren't going back to using again."

"Mom, I worked hard all day with Dad and I just wanted to get high and relax. You know, like what a lot of people do after a day's work. A lot of people will have a glass of wine or a beer. I wanted to do the same thing."

"But you can't do that! You should know, by now, you cannot drink or do any drugs, ever, without becoming addicted again. And, you got behind the wheel of a car. You could have killed someone or yourself. I just can't believe this. You were doing so well. Why?"

"I don't know, Mom. I'm sorry."

He'd been in recovery since mid-October. Three months. I was devastated.

After his arrest, things turned even more sour. He'd probably lose his license because of the DUI and he needed it for his job. We told him nothing was certain until his court date.

"Keep working," I told him, "Save as much as possible."

But he couldn't seem to forgive himself for his mistake and began to use in earnest; to help him feel better, I suppose. It was a trying time for me. His depression deepened, even though he was taking an antidepressant. He'd come so far. He'd been so positive and, due to one very stupid decision, he'd probably lose everything he'd come to love.

We saw the signs of drug abuse. He kept disappearing for long periods of time for no apparent reason. Though he continued working, he often showed up late. One day in March, his boss finally fired him. That was the last straw.

The next Saturday, a regular workday for him, he pretended to go to the group home. He was depressed.

The next day he did the same thing but before he left, he took $150 out of my pocketbook and headed straight for his dealer. He could not face us. He could not stand the pain he'd caused and decided he could no longer stand the pain he was in. He could no longer face life.

He used the money to buy drugs and spent the evening getting as high as possible, hoping he wouldn't wake up.

Once I realized my money was gone, I panicked. Eric didn't come home that night. I stayed up till sunrise, texting him and ringing his phone. Thoughts of burying him had been my constant companions for the past few years. Could the horror of burying my son soon become a reality? I felt sick.

I stayed home from work the next day, certain Eric was dead or near death. I expected a phone call from the police or a hospital and didn't want to be at work, when it came. As I kept texting him and ringing his phone, I planned his funeral in my mind. I cried.

Around 2:30 that afternoon, Eric texted, "I'm okay."

"Come home," I texted back.

"I can come home?"

"Yes, we need to talk."

My husband returned home from work around 4 p.m., unexpectedly early. I saw the upset in his face as well.

"Eric's on his way home," I said.

"We're having a family meeting," he said. "Jessica, Matthew, stick around."

When Eric walked in the front door at 5 p.m., he looked physically and emotionally exhausted; defeated. Unable to look at us, he kept his head down and stared at the floor.

"I'm using drugs," he said, "I took money from Mom's pocketbook. I lost my job."

A couple of nights earlier, he explained, he was held up at gunpoint.

"That's how I lost my phone," he said, tears streaming down his face, "I'm so fucked up. I'm so fucked up that having a gun pointed at my head can't stop me from using drugs. I'm so fucked up."

It broke my heart to see my son unable to control himself and his life.

At the family meeting, he cried as we each said what was on our minds. His sister really let him have it.

"I am ashamed of you and the way you act!" She said, "I am so disappointed, Eric."

"I just want you to be well again," Matthew said, "I want my brother back."

"I love you Eric, and I want you well," I said, "But I can't bear to live like this anymore."

His father echoed my sentiments.

In the end, we gave Eric two options. He could leave the house and be a drug addict and probably be in jail or dead within a month or he could get serious about getting better and go into a long-term treatment program.

"I'll do it," he said, his voice a whisper as he looked at the floor, "I'll go. I need the help."

Ten days later, Matthew, my husband, and I drove Eric to New Haven, Connecticut and checked him into a long-term treatment program.

Both times Eric had been in rehab, all his counselors said he did wonderfully. He came home excited, sharing all he'd learned from his experiences and proclaiming that sobriety meant more to him than anything.

At the family weekend in Texas, we were told the failure rate of an opiate addict after a thirty-day rehab stay was ninety percent.

When we had Eric stay in the Florida halfway house, we thought being in such a negative situation would motivate him to improve his circumstances. It didn't. It depressed and frustrated him more. When put in a less-than-perfect scenario, he clearly didn't know how to get himself out.

And why should he? He hadn't made many good decisions in his teen years or the years of his addiction.

Now, we knew, Eric needed more than thirty days of rehab because, with only that, he could not face the real world. For him, thirty days was only a start.

The philosophy at the Connecticut facility reassured me. You cannot put a recovering addict back into society after only thirty days of rehab and expect them to get a job, handle money, take on relationships, take care of a car, and master other responsibilities of daily life. That individual, the Connecticut rehab insisted, needs long-term support to sustain recovery.

Eric had been struggling with addiction for three years. Without extended help, though, he clearly could not sustain long-term recovery.

23. Connecticut
March 2011

As he did at the other treatment facilities, Eric called with the usual litany. He didn't have to be there. He could get better on his own.

I wasn't at all concerned. By then, I knew he was in withdrawal, depressed, and afraid of the future. At twenty-one, Eric still didn't control his own life and wouldn't for another year. I believed in the facility, too. I'd visited and talked with staff before admitting Eric. Unquestionably, it would meet his needs.

Once Eric settled in, he did amazingly well. His counselor gave me weekly progress reports. Eric's writing assignments were well thought out. After a couple of weeks, he was given a larger role in his group, too.

Eric's next call to me echoed the good news.

"Mom, I'm now responsible for choosing the topic for our group discussions. It makes me feel good I've been asked to do this," he said, "My counselor likes what I write. We have to do some reading and then write our reaction to what we've read. My counselor says I'm a good writer. I never thought I was good at writing."

"That's great," I said, "I'm very proud of you."

I visited Eric two weeks, after he settled in. I left my house at 9:30 a.m. and headed north on Route 95. As I entered the facility a little before noon, the residents swept and dusted and cleaned the kitchen. The chores were designed to instill discipline and pride.

A counselor sent a resident to tell Eric I was there. As we waited, we sat at the kitchen table.

"How is Eric doing?" I asked.

"He's doing great. He's really a nice kid," the counselor said, "He's very cooperative and always helpful."

Eric bounded the stairs, cutting our conversation short and engulfed me in one of his big bear hugs. He kissed me.

"Hi Mom, I'm glad you're here!" He said, smiling widely.

"It's great to see you," I said, reciprocating his hug, kiss, and enthusiasm.

In Phase one of the program, Eric could leave the facility with me for four hours. After his counselor approved our outing, we left. Eric directed me to a Chinese restaurant for lunch. We both liked Chinese food and sat down to a delicious meal.

"Eric, how is it going?"

"Mom, it's great. I really like my counselor. He's chill. I can talk to him. Everyone here has been an addict and I like that because they know what I've been through and what I'm going through to get better. Right now, the only thing I want to do is get better and make you proud of me."

He could hardly contain all his news.

"I've also found a sponsor. His name is Kyle and he is amazing. I was sitting in the back of the room during an AA meeting like I always do because I never like going. I was probably looking depressed and angry and this guy sits next to me and starts talking about addiction and recovery. He seemed to know what was on my mind and what I needed to hear. I listened and suddenly things made sense to me."

"I've never had things explained to me in that way or, who knows, maybe I just wasn't listening," he continued, "Kyle told me addiction is a disease and that I can't really help myself that I must begin to rely on a higher power to help me overcome it. I've heard that before but, somehow, it made more sense the way Kyle explained it."

"I can't believe it! Things are suddenly beginning to make sense. It's like a curtain of fog has lifted. Maybe, just maybe, I really can get better."

On he went. The more he talked, the more my heart warmed to see him so excited about recovery.

"Kyle put me on his email list and he sends all his sponsees a thought-provoking message each morning," Eric said, "I look forward to them. I've also learned about the history of AA and found out my home group is very close to the group's founder. I'm proud to be a part of such an organization and home group. My life seems so much better. I'm beginning to feel happy, really happy. I can't believe it."

"What are some of Kyle's messages?" I asked.

"Let me show you."

He took out his phone, scrolled, and read one to me, "Here's one from the other day. 'When I stopped living in the problem and began living in the answer, the problem went away.'"

The positive and genuine change in his attitude amazed me. This time he wanted to get better for himself, not just me.

After we ate, he led the way to a local park on Long Island Sound.

"Mom, I know how much you love the outdoors, so I thought you'd like this place. The rehab brought us here last week. Once a week, they bring us to a park or on a hike, somewhere outdoors. When we came here last week, I immediately thought of how much you'd love it."

We walked along the small beach and the rocky outcroppings along the park's southern edge. Then, we sat on the warm rocks. There wasn't a cloud in the sky. The temperature was perfect. Taking in the glassy sea and clear air and my euphoric son, I felt content.

Eric had to get back, so we left the park sooner than I would have wanted. Back at the rehab, I walked Eric in to make sure the counselor saw he had returned.

"Mom, thanks for coming! It was great to spend time with you. I love you, Mom. Thanks for everything."

We hugged.

"I'm glad I came. Thanks for planning such a nice day for me. I'll come and visit every other weekend, if that's okay with you?"

"I'd love that. I'll start planning for your next visit."

It was the best afternoon I'd had with Eric in a long time. I left New Haven with peace in my heart and the hope that Eric finally would succeed there.

After a month, he needed to come home for his DUI court appearance. Thinking about how the weekend could progress, made me nervous but it went well. Eric spent time with his sister and brother. We all hung around the house, watched movies, and played games. Not once did he ask to see his friends or use the car.

"Just sitting in my room feels so good," he said, "Even though I've made good friends in Connecticut, I'm tired of living in group settings. I like going into my room and lying on my bed all by myself."

To hear him talk about our house as a refuge soothed my soul.

At one point during his visit, I asked him a question that had been bothering me.

"Eric, why did you begin to take OxyContin? You must have known how highly addictive it was."

He looked at me, then at the ground.

"Because, Mom, I didn't care if I lived or died."

My brain screamed, *But I cared if you lived or died!* Why would he think it wouldn't matter if he died? I couldn't believe it.

On our drive back to Connecticut, Eric reflected on the weekend.

"I'm finally realizing I can't see my friends if I want to get better," he said, "I can't be around people who are still into partying. I can't allow myself to be tempted."

"You have to make a new circle of friends, which is what you're doing in Connecticut," I said, "You seem to like some of the guys you're living with. Continue to develop those friendships. You're all at the same place in life right now, so you should be able to support each other and be successful with your recoveries."

In mid-May, Eric moved into Phase Two of the program. I kept visiting every other weekend and he kept doing amazingly well. His progress impressed his counselors, who felt he was learning to deal with 'life on life's terms' – something they said every addict must learn to do without using drugs.

Though Eric showed substantial progress, I worried again. I'd been here before. My concern ran so deep, I wrote an email to his therapist.

"I want to let you know about my and my husband's concern for Eric, at this point in his treatment. We are both very proud of his progress and glad he has moved into Phase Two, where he'll be looking for employment. He seems to be taking his recovery very seriously this time and has spoken to me about things that bother him; things he never would admit were problems. With that said, we are very concerned because this is the point when Eric normally shoots himself in the foot.

"In the past, it seems that as soon as Eric enjoyed a bit of success, he always found a way to sabotage himself.

"It appears that whenever positive things happen, he finds a way to reverse the situation by using. I have shared my thoughts with Eric and he has, somewhat, agreed with my assessment.

"For Eric to keep moving forward in the positive direction he's going, he needs to feel he is worthy and deserving of a good and happy life. I ask that you please speak to him about this pattern he falls into and get him to understand he is just as good and deserving as anyone else in this world.

"In a recent conversation, he called himself a failure. I tried to tell him otherwise but I don't think he believed me. Please speak to him about feeling like a failure and give him constructive ways to work through this.

"We really want Eric to succeed and we also know he is capable of so much. We see it and just about everyone that meets Eric sees it. Now, we need Eric to see it.

"If he cannot see the goodness in himself and forgive himself for his past errors, we are very worried he'll use them as an excuse to go back to drugs. Honestly, I will not be able to handle him falling backwards again. Please work on these things with Eric."

The counselor replied, saying the last time he'd met with Eric, they'd discussed his feelings of unworthiness. He told me Eric had begun to think more about it, which he found potentially dangerous, since he only saw Eric once a week. He wrote,

"People with low self-esteem get caught in a pattern of needing and seeking approval. Then, when they get it, they feel the pressure of having to maintain it or live up to it. The approval places the person on the radar, as opposed to below it.

"As an adult, a person has an ideal to live up to and is evaluated in almost every aspect of life by peers, bosses, girlfriends or boyfriends, parents, professors, and more. This allows for many opportunities to confirm one's feeling of being less than or a failure.

"A kid is expected to play and be precocious. An adult is expected to enter a stable relationship, find a career, act mature, solve problems, and so on. Consequently, for many, recognition by others, although sought and temporarily fulfilling, becomes an expectation."

After getting my email, he decided to check in with Eric between sessions via phone to remind him of things they had discussed.

His response confirmed my own thoughts about Eric's behavior; he didn't feel good enough to accept happiness and love. I traced the thought straight back to his being adopted. His birth mother gave him away, making him feel, on some fundamental level, undeserving of any love and, perhaps, even unlovable. He often spoke negatively about the people who loved him, including me. He also did everything in his power to push away the people, who loved him, the most. That pattern only seemed to apply to his family, though. He always had a very close circle of friends throughout his childhood and High School.

I suppose his friends were his refuge from the expectations his family held for him. Although I never pressured Eric to be perfect, I encouraged him to do the best he could and use his God-given talents, just like a parent should.

After all, Eric had showed us many gifts. Everything seemed to come easily to him. So, why did he feel frightened about using his talents and being his best self? Why did he find others' expectations of him unreasonable when he should have had those expectations for himself?

The questions had floated through my mind for many years. I was relieved a therapist was finally discussing them with Eric.

Entering Phase Two meant that Eric moved into another house and changed his routine. He had more free time for job hunting or researching his next educational step.

The thought of free time filled me with anxiety. Though he was still well monitored and met with his counselor and therapist regularly, he'd be on his own sometimes. Was he ready? Could he handle a temptation put in front of him? Would anything trigger his memory of drug use?

Although his newfound freedom frightened me, I accepted it as part of the healing and recovery process. I forced myself to stay calm.

During one of my visits, we talked about volunteer work, which the program required.

"I don't like the idea of volunteering," Eric said, "I feel I should get paid for anything I do. Mom, I don't have a penny to my name. I'm getting impatient about not having any money. If I want to move on in life, I need to make and save money."

"Volunteering can have a different value," I said, "Helping others can make you feel good about yourself. Don't dismiss it. It can help you."

"Yeah, I get it, but I'm twenty-one and I really need to start making money. How will I ever get ahead in life if I don't have any?"

I understood his frustration but the idea of money in his hands troubled me. It was a way to buy drugs. I told him that.

"I know, Mom. So far, I've only bought drugs with any money I've made. I've worked fifty to sixty hours a week as a cook at a restaurant and don't have a penny to show for it. I made $150 a day in tips waiting tables and I don't have a penny to show for it."

"I used to have a bank account but I emptied that out when my drug habit became too bad. I should probably have at least thirty thousand dollars in savings, at this point. I can't believe how stupid I've been and how much money and time I've wasted. I can't help but feel ashamed."

Ultimately, he decided he'd like volunteering in the rehab's kitchen. He still entertained the idea of going to culinary school and thought the experience would help him. I approached his counselor about a kitchen job.

In the meantime, we kept Eric on a very short monetary leash. He learned to do without. He smoked less, for instance, and grubbed cigarettes from other residents.

Happily, he rarely asked for money. The few times he did, I gave him twenty dollars. I was afraid to give him more.

The first time he went to rehab, we were very considerate of his needs, buying him a carton of cigarettes and giving him fifty dollars in spending money, though we didn't know if he'd need any of it. The second time, in Florida, I'd slipped him twenty-five dollars before he walked through airport security.

We both knew that if he really wanted drugs, he'd find a way. They're everywhere. We raised him in a semirural area. If he found them there, he certainly could find them in New Haven. But why make it easy?

Soon after our talk about volunteering, the rehab approved Eric's request to volunteer in its kitchen a few days a week.

"Remember, volunteering doesn't mean you stop looking for a paying job," I reminded him.

I sensed he wasn't looking too hard, though. I also wasn't convinced he really knew how to land a job. He'd gotten all his previous ones through friends. He'd never had to interview for a position and didn't appear comfortable going into stores and talking to strangers. I reinforced that's exactly what he had to do, though. Was he listening to me? I wasn't sure.

He did well volunteering in the kitchen and was told that they might hire a new employee. Wanting that position, Eric put in even more hours, which didn't allow him to look for another job. He'd given himself a goal. That was good but it frustrated me. I just wanted him to get a job.

In our phone conversations, I told him to keep applying at other places.

"Nothing is certain, Eric," I said.

But he was confident he'd get the kitchen post.

"Mom, I like the people, who work in the kitchen, and that's important to me," he said, "So, I'm willing to put in more time as a volunteer so that maybe they will hire me. I'm willing to take the chance, that's all."

While in Phase Two, Eric started to take better care of his body, for which, I was grateful. Over the past three years, he'd abused it with drugs and food. He'd gained forty-five pounds since high school, which didn't help his already low self-esteem.

"Mom, I hate my round face," he constantly told me, "When I look in the mirror, that's all I see; my big, fat, round face and my double chin."

"I bet that if you lost some weight you'd lose some of the roundness in your face and your double chin," I told him, "It's not easy to lose weight but you can do, it if you put your mind to it."

"Do you think I'll lose the weight in my face?"

"Probably, but if you don't, we can think about going to a plastic surgeon if it bothers you that much," I said, "But lose the weight first. It might do the trick."

During another visit in Phase Two, he talked more about the weight he'd gained.

"I guess gaining weight gave me a reason to really hate who I am," he said, "As an addict, you hate yourself on the inside. You have to. If you loved yourself, you wouldn't do the things to your body that an addict does. Now, with all the weight I've gained, all I have to do is look in the mirror for a reason to hate myself on the outside, too. I guess you could say that what I see in the mirror confirms what I feel on the inside."

I still didn't understand why Eric was so down on himself. He was talented and smart. I hoped he'd lose weight, though, and feel better about himself.

"Self-hate and internal pain are two traits an addict has to have," he explained, "Getting high makes you feel good, so you don't have to be in pain and you can see yourself as beautiful. Then, the high wears off and you need to get high again, so you don't have to be the person you've learned to hate so much."

He and another kid in Phase Two started the Insanity® Workout together. Eric lost some weight immediately. I hoped feeling better about his body would help him like what was underneath.

Every time I visited, Eric had lost more weight. It was obvious and so was his growing self-confidence.

During one of my visits, he said, "I can't believe that two months ago I tried to end my life. I'm beginning to feel lucky I've been given a second chance."

That was music to my ears.

24. You Can't Come Home
May–June 2011

After a month in the Phase Two house, Eric proceeded into Phase Three, which required a move into a new house.

After the move, he called me.

"Mom, I love this place! You should see the apartment I'm living in. I have a kitchen, so I can cook my own meals now and it is beautiful. It's right on the river. I love this place!"

Sharing with five other guys didn't matter to him. He was just happy. I was, too, but paired with wariness. Phase Three meant even more freedom for Eric.

There were still rules. He had to stay in contact with his counselor, work or volunteer, regularly see his therapist and psychiatrist, and attend a certain number of AA or NA meetings a week.

Beyond that, he was free to come and go as he pleased.

I kept coming biweekly to spend quality time. On every trip, we also bought groceries to sustain him until my next visit.

Eric had an account at the rehab, into which, we could have deposited money but we only did that once in Phase Two. Even then, we only put in enough for a bus pass to get him into the city to look for a job.

At that point, I still didn't want to give him too much money. To me, cash meant drugs.

In Phase Three, though, I saw he needed cash in between my visits to get food, do laundry, and buy more bus passes. I broke down and deposited $150 into his account. All of his counselors told me my approach was appropriate.

An important goal remained. Eric needed to support himself.

Usually my Saturday visits were very pleasant. We'd find a nice place for lunch, talk, walk around the city, and go shopping. At times, Eric showed his frustration with life. We usually were able to talk through his issue. Normally, by the time I left, he was calm.

During one visit, Eric made an announcement.

"Mom, I think I can go back home now. I've been sober for four months. I can handle it."

My heart skipped a beat.

"Oh, no. You can't come back home. Every time you come back home, you use. There is no way you can live at home anymore."

"But, Mom, I *know* I can handle it this time. I know I won't be tempted. I miss not being home and, sometimes, I just get tired with everything I need to do.

"Sometimes I don't want to have to follow the rules," he said, "Sometimes, I don't want a counselor, therapist, psychiatrist, and what seems like a hundred other people in my business telling me what to do. Even though I have a lot of freedom at this point; sometimes, I just want to be left alone and live my life the way I want to."

"Also, I don't feel you should be spending so much money on me. You're using my college fund. What if I decide I want to go to college or culinary school? How will I pay for that?"

Panic tore through my insides.

"Eric, you can't come back home. When you came to Connecticut, you agreed to stay in Phase Three for at least six months. Even after that, I don't think you should come home. There are too many triggers. Think about what you want to do after you're done here. Do you want to stay in New Haven or go back to school? But the school shouldn't be in Northern New Jersey."

During another visit, he talked about how difficult recovery was.

"My counselor tells me I must learn to deal with life on life's terms. I know he's right and I'm able to do that most of the time," he said, "But, sometimes, things just get me crazy. I've opened up to my counselor and talked to him about the things that bother me and he gives me ways to handle my frustrations. It's hard, though. It's hard to deal with things without drugs, when you know drugs can make you feel better so quickly; at least, until you end up back in rehab."

He paused and chuckled at what he'd just said.

"Mom, I absolutely know I will not do this again," he went on, "If I relapse, I will not go back to rehab. I don't know what will happen to me but I don't want to find myself back in a rehab situation ever again. I really hope I can do this but I also know the odds are stacked against me. This is my third time in treatment and each time has been very difficult."

"I know that if I do this and stay drug free the rest of my life, it will be the most difficult thing that I will ever have done. Don't get me wrong, I'm very proud of myself and don't plan on using but why does it have to be so damn hard?"

His words upset me to the point of tears. I didn't know how to respond. *Why would he tell me this? Is he thinking he will relapse?*

"Mom, I didn't mean to get you upset," he said, "It's just that it is so hard, really hard." He looked at me with concern, "Come on, let's find a place you can have a cup of tea. I don't want you to leave upset."

We found a Dunkin' Donuts®. He had coffee, I had tea. I warmed my hands on the brew for a few moments before I could speak to him.

"Eric, I know this is hard for you but you *need* to do this. You know addiction has almost destroyed your life and you can't let that happen again. You need to be successful, so you can have your life back. Always remember that you have so much to live for and a family that loves you."

"I know but it's just so damn hard," he repeated, "It really is."

He talked about other things, mundane matters, but I couldn't focus on the conversation. I was too upset.

25. Life Is Good
Summer 2011

Two weeks later, I sat in the front seat as my husband, Jessica, and I headed to Connecticut. My husband drove. Jessica sat in the back. I was happy for my sunglasses. I didn't want them to see me holding back tears. It was Eric's birthday, July 31st, and he was twenty-two, the age he swore he'd never reach.

When we arrived at his apartment building, he was waiting for us in the parking lot. I sprung from the car and ran to him.

"Eric, you made it!" I exclaimed, "You're twenty-two."

He gave me a bear hug. I hugged him back and kissed him.

"Yeah, Mom, and I'm sober, too."

We'd come to celebrate this milestone with him, leaving the agenda for the day up to him.

For once, he was going to forget his diet and dine at one of his favorite Italian restaurants on Wooster Street, New Haven's Little Italy. After lunch, we took pictures in a small park down the street before driving to downtown New Haven and walking around the city.

I kept taking pictures. The day was special to me and I wanted pictures to help me remember it.

Even so, I was still on pins and needles about Eric's job prospects. He'd been volunteering in the rehab's kitchen since June, harboring the hope he'd be hired as kitchen help. In late July, the kitchen manager gave his notice. Instantly, Eric wanted that job.

The news had been good and bad. I was glad Eric had set himself a goal and put energy into impressing the boss but nervous about what would happen, if he didn't get the job. Would he use?

I encouraged him even as I tempered his expectations. He listened but remained certain he'd get the job. We waited.

One weekend, he helped host a parent information session. Wanting to show off his new culinary skills, he asked me to visit on a Sunday, instead of Saturday. After the event, he showed me the platters he'd helped prepare. They were done with an artistic flair I didn't know Eric possessed. One featured many types of artistically arranged cheeses intermixed with red grapes.

In early August, an ecstatic Eric called.

"Guess who the new kitchen manager at the rehab is?"

"You?" I asked.

"Yes, me!"

I was relieved and very proud.

That month, my nieces threw a surprise birthday party for my sister and brother-in-law in Rhode Island. Eric asked us to pick him up on our way, so he could come. Although I knew Eric loved the family, he hadn't always made himself available for celebrations. Due to work or drugs, he'd missed many family functions. The request made me happy.

Everyone at the party was delighted to see Eric. My mother, who'd accompanied me on two visits to Connecticut, was the only other person from my extended family, who'd seen Eric since he moved to New England. All weekend, he reconnected with his cousins.

I beamed with pride for my son. He continued his recovery and was setting and attaining personal goals. It seemed like my beautiful boy was finding his way back.

26. Making Amends
September 2011

In September Matthew, my husband, and I drove to New Haven at Eric's request. He wanted to officially apologize for the problems he'd caused the family and make amends. Jessica couldn't make the date, so she had visited a week earlier.

We arrived around one o'clock and, immediately, went to Eric's and my favorite burger place. I ordered my usual turkey burger and Eric, Matthew, and my husband ordered from their selection of gourmet burgers.

Conversation came easily and revolved mostly around work, food, and sports. I smiled and sat quietly as the guys talked animatedly. My husband and Matthew visited Eric every six weeks, usually on one of my off weeks, so I hadn't witnessed their reconnection.

After lunch, we strolled the city and returned to Eric's apartment. Since the fall afternoon was sunny and crisp, we sat on the back porch. I took in Eric's neighborhood from a different vantage point. His house had a narrow and grassy backyard that needed mowing.

The surrounding houses; each had the same-sized backyard and small back porch. Though the houses were close together, the neighborhood was very quiet.

We chatted until the conversation turned serious. Standing and leaning against the porch railing, facing us, Eric spoke, "Mom, Dad, Matthew, I wanted you to come up today to apologize for everything I've done since becoming addicted to drugs. I realize now that my addiction has not been easy for you and I'm really sorry for all I've put you through."

"I know that right now I can't make amends and pay you for anything I've taken from you but when I get more financially stable, I promise I will. Again, I'm really sorry."

I moved toward Eric and hugged him.

"Thanks for the apology and wanting to make amends," I said, "But, right now, the most important thing is for you to work on your recovery. It's okay if you can't financially make amends right now. You can pay us when you are able to. That will be okay."

"Eric, I'm proud of you wanting to make amends," my husband said, "But like your mother, I believe you need to worry now about getting better. When you are able, you can do what you need to make amends."

"Thanks, I really want to make amends," Eric said, "But, what I want, most of all is your forgiveness. I'm ashamed of all the things I've done. I'm sorry for the pain I've caused you. I've asked forgiveness from Jesus and he has forgiven me. I hope you can, too."

"We forgive you, Eric," I said, "Just continue to get better. We just want you to get better, that's all."

Matthew let us do most of the talking.

"It's okay," he told his brother, "We all just want you to get better, like Mom said."

We each hugged and kissed Eric and sat on the porch for another half hour before making our way to the front of the house and saying our goodbyes.

My heart burst with happiness. I was proud of Eric's progress. My son was climbing out of the hell of addiction.

27. A Beautiful Day
October 2011

I especially looked forward to visiting Connecticut, around my birthday. Eric wanted to celebrate with me. The drive was gorgeous, the day brilliant, and I smiled the whole way up.

"Happy birthday, Mom!" he shouted, when I arrived at his apartment.

I enjoyed our embrace. After he let go, I stood back, awed by the transformation of the past six months. He'd grown out his black hair, which was thick and wavy. He'd lost thirty pounds. His face was thinning; I saw his cheekbones. With the new definition to his face, his eyes looked bigger.

Besides the physical change, he'd become self-assured. He walked with his head high and exuding confidence. He'd become the young man I always knew he could be.

"You look great, Mom," he said before leaving his kitchen and returning with a bouquet of flowers. He handed them to me.

"Happy Birthday, Mom!"

"Thank you! They're beautiful!"

Then, he handed me a card with sparkles and rhinestones on the front. Its sentiment was simple, "Happy Birthday. Wishing you a spectacular day."

Inside was a note:

Mom,

Happy Birthday! I want to thank you for everything you have done for me and all the love you have shown me.

My life has changed remarkably in the last six months and I could have never done it without your love and all of your support. I know it has been a rocky road but I am here today to tell you that my life has turned for the better and I have never felt so alive and full inside before.

With the help of you and God, I feel that we have beaten this together. I am so grateful and thankful to have you in my life. I love and care for you more than words could ever express or explain.

Thank you for everything and Happy Birthday!

Emotional, I hugged him.

"Thank you for such a beautiful card," I said.

"So, what do you want to do?"

"I wouldn't mind walking into the city for ice cream."

"We'll do it, if that's what you want," he said, "Today we do what *you* want."

The day was perfect; no wind, a slight chill, and a beautiful blue sky. We walked past the wood-framed houses that lined Eric's street, all of them close together with very small front yards. Some were unkempt. Others were well maintained with gardens of mums. Closer to the corner were larger homes on much bigger pieces of property.

Eric pointed out a deli with a patio and tables in front, that he and his buddies frequented for coffee or sandwiches.

I understood why he liked the neighborhood. It was a great place for a young person starting out; enough room to enjoy yourself and yet, close to all the conveniences of downtown New Haven.

"Mom, I've learned so much since being in Connecticut," he said, "I understand why I became a drug addict and I know I can turn my life around with the help of God."

"Really?" I said, "You've been to a lot of AA meetings in the past three years and you've heard about the need for a Higher Power before. Why this sudden excitement?"

"I've learned I was born this way and, no matter how life turned out for me, I, eventually, would have become an addict. My brain is different and, yeah, maybe, I could have made different choices but making good choices was always difficult for me. I see the negative side to life and never felt good about myself. Now, I do."

He seemed free, excited, but I was again shocked.

"But, Eric, why didn't you feel good about yourself?" I quickly replied, "You're such a smart person and you were good at everything you did."

"But that is *not* what my brain tells me, Mom. You might think I'm smart and I might be smart like you say, but my brain doesn't let me think that and nothing you or anyone else says can convince me of it."

"I also never thought people liked me when I was younger or when I was older, for that matter."

"Why would you think *that*?"

"When I was younger, I thought I had to make people laugh. I sat on the bus on the way to school thinking of ways to make people laugh, so they'd like me. Remember that joke book I had?"

"Yes. I also remember how amazed your father and I were that you memorized just about every joke in it. You used to tell those jokes, at the dinner table."

"I memorized all of them to make people laugh, so they would like me."

We'd all thought being funny was part of Eric's personality. I'd had no idea he thought he *had* to be funny.

"I also hated being the only Asian kid around," he said, "I hated being Asian in a white world."

When he was little, he and Jessica were welcomed by anyone we met. I remembered only one incident when someone mocked his appearance. If that happened regularly, he never told his teachers, his coaches, or me.

"I always felt being different was a barrier to my success," Eric went on, "And, I didn't like looking different from all my friends. Usually, I was the only Asian kid wherever I went. In High School, my friends sometimes made fun of me. Even though, I knew they were just kidding, it really bothered me."

There was never any indication Eric felt anything but proud of his looks when he was younger. In High School, he was very popular and had a girlfriend. I was glad he was opening up but I wished he'd talked about these issues at the time. He could have talked to me or one of his therapists.

"Does it bother you that you're adopted?"

"No, it doesn't bother me," he said, hesitating a moment, "I guess that, maybe, it bothers me a little."

"I'm glad to hear you say that because I always thought being adopted was a problem for you. You do know that your birth mother couldn't take care of you and that by allowing you to be adopted, she gave you a chance for a better life."

He looked at the ground, glanced sideways at me, and smiled slightly.

"If you had stayed in South Korea, Eric, your career options would have been limited, once you left the orphanage. Please, always remember that you are loved. I love you. Everyone in the family loves you. Your friends love you."

He didn't look up or say a word.

I changed the subject.

"Do you consider yourself an alcoholic as well as a drug addict?"

"Yes."

I was relieved. I was worried he might substitute alcohol for drugs.

He looked upward and shook his hands in front of him.

"I wish I could describe to you how drugs take hold of an addict's brain," he said, "And how it feels to be an addict and how hard it is to stay away from the drugs."

120

"I'm not sure since I've never been addicted but I think it might go something like this. I am invited to three parties over a weekend, one on Friday night and two all day Saturday and Sunday. I decide I'm going to drink as much as I want because that's how I've decided to enjoy myself. On Monday morning when I wake up, I feel so lousy that I swear I'll never do something like that again. You, on the other hand, being an addict, would wake up and instantly want more."

"That's right!" he shouted, "My brain would have wanted to keep drinking or doing drugs. It won't let me stop, even if it knows I should. When I was doing drugs, Mom, they were all I could think about. It's called having a mental obsession with the drugs. Getting beyond the mental obsession is the hardest thing about recovery."

I couldn't believe he agreed so heartily with what I'd said. Mental obsession was a new thought; something he'd never discussed before.

"I think you started using drugs and drinking too much in High School because sports didn't work out the way you expected. What do you think?"

"I don't know. When I was younger, the fact I was good at any sport made me feel good about myself but I don't think that not doing well in High School sports made me turn to drugs."

"Maybe, if sports in High School worked more in my favor, I wouldn't have turned to drugs so early. But, at some point, when life became difficult, I would have turned to drugs. Drugs made me feel good about myself, just like sports did, when I was younger.

"Drugs made me feel so good, Mom. They allowed me to feel loved and they allowed me to love myself."

I still struggled to comprehend his negative self-image.

"What about after you became addicted? Did the drugs give you the same feeling?"

"The initial high still made me feel good but the fact I was addicted and could only think about getting drugs to feed my habit counteracted the positive feeling," he explained, "Once the addiction is bad, life becomes unbearable. As an addict, all you can think of is how and where you're going to get your next fix; the mental obsession."

"You know I missed a lot of family functions, Mom. That was because I always had to get drugs. I'd do anything to get the drugs I needed. I'm ashamed of some of the things I did but I've asked God for forgiveness and I've received forgiveness from Him."

"Mom, I'm ready to move on. It feels good to be free of such a burden. I began to use because I hated myself and, now, I don't hate myself anymore."

Oh my God, that was his struggle! Self-hatred.

In High School, he always told me life was a struggle and I could never understand how that could be. He never wanted for food, clothing, or a friend to play with. What struggle? Now, I knew. His struggle was on the inside.

"You know, Mom, Matthew is my hero."

"Matthew, your brother, is your hero? Why?"

"Matthew loves himself. He doesn't have to pretend to be someone else when he's around other people. He's comfortable with who he is. I have a lot to learn from him."

I was touched that he thought so highly of his younger brother, I almost cried. Matthew and Eric were only two years apart. They'd been close growing up and, like many siblings, had grown apart. Perhaps, they'd become close again as adults.

At the ice cream parlor, I ordered my favorite, a cup of cookies and cream and Eric ordered his chocolate chip cookie cough in a cone. We found a place to sit.

"Mom, none of this is your fault or Dad's fault. You and Dad did a great job as parents. You couldn't have been better. The fact I'm a drug addict has everything to do with me and nothing to do with you or Dad. You raised the three of us the same way and only I'm fucked up."

It was hard not to cry into my ice cream. A parent with an addicted child always has to wonder what they did wrong. I suppose I already knew it wasn't our fault but it was good to hear it from him.

"I'm grateful for everything you've done for me and for sticking by me through all this," he said, "Mom, you really are my best friend."

I was taken aback but honored. I leaned against him and rested my head on his shoulder.

"You're my best friend, too," I said.

We finished our ice creams and began the twenty-five-minute walk back to his place, talking the whole time. Seeing him happy and at peace was wonderful. Having such a deep conversation with him was thrilling.

Since he began his struggle, I'd often said, "Everyone loves Eric, except Eric."

Maybe, he finally was beginning to love himself. Maybe, he finally was finding the inner peace that had always eluded him. I felt elated. As we walked and talked, I held onto his arm and squeezed it. *My son is happy!* He was able to speak about things that had weighed heavily in his heart.

He also talked about the future, which meant he thought he had one. My heart sang.

28. He's Home
November–December 2011

Eric talked about moving out of the program. He'd been working full time, handling his expenses, cooking, doing laundry, and taking care of himself for a few months, seemingly with ease.

Six kids, he knew from the program, shared an apartment. A room was becoming available. They asked Eric to join them.

He had agreed to stay in Phase Three for at least six months, though, and I wanted him to stay put at least until January. Even though he seemed positive and made great strides, I wasn't certain he should move out on his own. If he stayed until January, he'd have more money saved and another two months of sobriety under his belt.

But I also told him that it was his decision.

He decided to stay in the program until the end of the year. Later he told me why; one of the six kids wasn't taking his sobriety seriously. Eric didn't want to tempt himself.

At times, when he became frustrated about something in his life, I asked him, "Are you thinking of doing something stupid?"

His reply was always the same, "No, Mom, I am never going back to using drugs. I am done with that."

I was always glad to hear him talk about his commitment. Even so, as his mother and after all we'd been through, I wouldn't trust what I saw for a long time.

I constantly prayed for him, beseeching Jesus, "Shine your light before him and show him the way but don't let go of his hand, yet. And, Lord, you have my permission to smack him if he should ever think about using drugs again."

In the fall, Eric prepared to get his driver's license back. He took a class, got insurance, registered his car, and installed an ignition interlock device. He arranged and paid for everything, without our assistance.

The Friday before Thanksgiving, I drove to New Haven to pick him up, so he could take the required class in New Jersey, which ran all weekend. Driving two hours on a Friday after work was exhausting, especially on Route 95 in Connecticut. Even so, I'd come to enjoy our rides back and forth.

After forty-five minutes on the road heading back to New Jersey Friday evening, we stopped at an Italian restaurant north of Stamford. We shared a Margherita pizza, which he rated on presentation, taste, and freshness of ingredients. He'd become quite the connoisseur.

"Mom, I think I want to work at the rehab kitchen for maybe another year," he said, enjoying the pie, "And, then, I want to go to culinary school."

"That would be great. Have you thought about which one?"

"No."

"If you think you want to begin next September or January, start looking into schools now. I don't know how competitive they are. Also, do you want to go to a school like the Culinary Institute of America, where you can earn a four-year college degree? Or do you want to go to a school that won't take four years?"

"I don't think I want to go to school for four years but I'm not sure. I need to think about that."

"I'm glad you're thinking about your next step. When you find schools that interest you, we'll go look at them. I'd love to do that with you."

"I know, Mom, and I'd like you to come with me. Thanks for everything. You have really stuck by me through all of this. Thanks."

"You're welcome. I'm just glad you're doing so well and that you seem so happy."

It was dark by the time I dropped him off Sunday night, in front of the house, where he lived. We took his luggage out of the car, stood on the sidewalk, and hugged.

"Well, you're home."

"Yeah, Mom, I am. This is my home now. I like New Haven and I've made a lot of friends here."

We said our goodbyes and I drove away. By the time, I reached the entrance ramp to Route 91, I was crying. Tears streamed down my face. *Why was I crying?* I should have been glad Eric was happily living in New Haven. I should have been glad he no longer talked about living in New Jersey. I should have been happy with all the progress he'd made. And, I was!

As I continued onto Route 95 and passed through New Haven, I realized what was happening. For Eric to be well and stay well, I had to let him go. I had to let him stay in Connecticut or anywhere else he decided to live. Although I'd already come to that conclusion, hearing him say he'd found a new home stung me.

At that moment, I knew I'd always need to drive a distance to see him and that he could never live nearby. In a sense, I'd lost my son. My home could never be his home again.

29. A Christmas Visit
December 2011

Eric drove himself home for Christmas but couldn't stay for Christmas Day. He had to cook for the rehab residents. He came home Friday night and stayed until after dinner Christmas Eve.

It was wonderful having him home for the holidays.

On Christmas Eve morning, I drove him to the lab for his routine Hepatitis B blood work, before stopping for a bagel breakfast. That afternoon, we exchanged gifts. My three children chipped in and got me a warm pair of slippers and a new teapot. Eric seemed especially happy with the teapot.

"I picked it out for you, Mom," he said, "I chose the nicest, most expensive one they had because you deserve the best."

His comment made me smile, as I looked at the teapot and placed it on my stove.

We, then, gave Eric the gifts he would have received Christmas morning. He liked everything I bought for him; a buffalo sweater, a pair of jeans, and a season of *NCIS*. I also gave him a bag of spices and oils along with cooking utensils and a set of pots to encourage his good eating habits and his interest in cooking.

"Mom, I love everything you gave me and I can't wait to cook with all these new spices and oils and to use the pots." He inspected the spices and each pot, "These pots are great. They are exactly what I wanted."

At one o'clock in the afternoon, we went to my sister's house. My family is Italian, so we always got together on Christmas Eve for a fish dinner. My family, who hadn't seen Eric since August, marveled at his new look and demeanor. He'd grown out his hair. Wavy and black, it covered his ears. He wore a pair of jeans with the new sweater and plaid shirt his brother and sister had given him for Christmas.

He stood tall, smiled, and talked easily to everyone.

My brother pulled him aside, talked to him about God, and gave him a Bible. And, my mother couldn't stop telling him how wonderful he looked. She was in awe at the transformation.

At one point during our celebration, I sat across the room from Eric and just looked at him. I called over to him, got his attention, and held up my camera to take a picture. He smiled and waved as I took the picture.

I continued to stare for a few minutes, not believing I was looking at my son; a confident, self-assured young man. *We did it. Eric is okay*, I said to myself. *I have my son back.*

30. Moving Out
January 2012

Eric moved out of the rehab on January 1, 2012. He stayed in a halfway house for a few weeks, before joining the five kids, who'd offered him a room. The kid, who'd worried him, had moved out. Living with the others was much cheaper than staying at the halfway house and Eric wanted to save money.

I was okay with his decision because he'd thought it through. Also, I didn't have a lot of faith in halfway houses, since our experience in Florida.

Every other weekend, I visited him, as usual. With each visit, he seemed more and more excited about living on his own and his prospects for the future.

Eric shared the bottom floor of the apartment with two of the five other guys and had a bedroom and bathroom of his own. They shared a kitchen and common area. The other three lived upstairs.

He outfitted his bathroom and bought a comforter for his bed and a used couch. During one visit, we purchased a table for his TV. His little place delighted him. It was fun to see him so happy and responsible for himself.

On January 8, his father and I visited and took him out early for his airplane day; the day he arrived in this country and became our son. It was like his second birthday and we'd celebrated it every year, since his arrival.

I visited him later in January and, again, we had a great time together. We went to an Asian market down the street from his house and then to a deli that carried specialty foods. Eric loved perusing the aisles for interesting and different foods.

With each visit, I felt more and more proud of him and how he'd turned his life around. He'd been to the depths of hell, where addiction leads, and he'd returned. Addiction affects everyone who loves the addict. I felt a great weight lift off my shoulders.

The worst was past. Finally, we could move forward. I found myself walking with my head held high. I felt great about my life.

During a few of my visits, kids in recovery had called Eric for encouragement. He talked to them calmly and told them two things; it definitely gets easier and the struggle for sobriety is worth it.

"With sobriety, life gets better," he said.

Helping others made him feel good about himself. For a time, he volunteered at a detox once a week. He told me how great it felt to speak to people about recovery.

In January, by invitation, he spoke at a large AA meeting in Massachusetts. People, who heard him speak, couldn't believe how eloquent he was about his addiction and recovery. Later, when I heard a recording of his speech, I felt such pride.

Eric spoke about his four-year journey to sobriety, made all the more difficult by his resistance to the twelve steps.

"I was stuck in this place where I thought AA didn't work," he told the crowd, recounting one of the lowest points in his addiction; his months in Florida.

He also talked about the night he met Kyle, his Connecticut sponsor, at a meeting. Eric said he'd sat in the back, not absorbing what he needed to fill the hole in his soul. Until his sponsor, who sat down next to him, explained the steps in a way he understood. He called it his moment of enlightenment.

First, he said, he learned there are two kinds of drinkers; problem drinkers and real alcoholics.

"Kyle told me a problem drinker is someone whose problem goes away, when you remove the alcohol because the alcohol was the problem," he explained, "Whatever the reason they have to stop drinking, whether it be the threat of losing their job or their wife or their health, they stop."

But a real alcoholic is another type of person.

"With the real alcoholic that the big book speaks upon," Eric said, "You take that alcohol away, you take those drugs away and life gets worse."

"It gets worse on the inside," he explained, "Even if things are better on the outside, even if a new girlfriend comes along or there's money in the bank."

"Inside," he said, "That feeling comes again that dying feeling because the substance was a 'solution' to a bigger problem."

"My problem has always been living life," Eric said, "I have a problem with life, not a problem with alcohol."

He spoke of the phony solution leading to addiction and the one and only real solution, which he, at long last, had embraced.

"We try to overcomplicate the shit out of this but it's really simple," Eric said. "I've looked everywhere for a solution but nothing could ever fill this hole like God does. No human power can relieve our alcoholism."

129

"I always thought that I was going to do it and my mother and father always thought that they were going to do it. At first, I really thought that it was going to be my network and my sponsor that was going to do it, but my sponsor is human. My sober network is made up of all humans. God is the only one, if I seek him by serving others."

He still doesn't understand God, he told the gathering, but he works the steps; the only way he knows to fill his void.

"I feel that presence," he said, "And it's never ever, ever been there before."

My beautiful boy was a man; a sober and free man, who walked with the Lord.

One day, toward the end of January, as I drove home from work, a bolt of electricity shot through my body. A horrible thought entered my mind, *this is usually when the trap door opens.*

I couldn't believe such a thought could come to mind with things going so well. I countered the thought with another one, *No, not this time. We, Eric and I, have finally done it. There is no way anything bad can happen. Eric is well. My son is back.*

31. Surprise
February 2012

We decided that Eric would come home to New Jersey the second weekend in February, instead of my driving up to New Haven. He still enjoyed coming home and lazing around the house and I liked having him.

I'd forgotten that we'd made dinner plans with friends for Saturday night, though, so we told him to come home the following weekend instead. That way, we could go out to dinner, as a family Saturday night.

He surprised us by coming home the second weekend, anyway.

I was working on the computer in the family room, when he walked in around 1:30, yelling, "Mommy! I'm home."

I jumped up, ran into the kitchen, and hugged him.

"You came home?! I thought you weren't coming."

"Mom, sometimes, I just want to come home. Even though I love where I live, I miss everyone."

"New Haven is only two hours away," I replied, "So you can come home, any-time you want."

All afternoon, we were home alone, so we sat around and talked. He was beginning to read books, including one entitled *Basketball Junkie*. I was glad he was reading but concerned about his selection.

"Do you think you should be reading a book about addiction, so early in your recovery?"

"Mom, it's a good book. It's about a guy with a drug habit, who played professional basketball and basketball overseas."

"I'm still not sure if you should be reading books about addiction at such an early point in your recovery."

"Mom, it's okay. He never talks positively about drugs. He just talks about how they almost destroyed his life."

"I don't know, Eric. I'm still not sure."

We stood at the island in the kitchen, where I helped him fill out an application for a credit card. He'd discovered his credit rating was zero and was serious about changing it.

While we filled out the application, he surprised me.

"Mom, I needed Daddy more when I was growing up," he said.

Even though he and his father had a strained relationship over the years, he'd never made such an admission.

"I know. I tried to tell your father that, but he couldn't understand what I was trying to tell him," I said, "I'm sorry. I wish I could have made him understand what you needed."

"It's okay, Mom. I forgive him. I understand now that Dad did what he thought he had to do to give us a good life. He worked hard and provided well for us and that's what he thought being a good father was. When I was younger, I thought he loved me only because I was good at baseball."

"Your father didn't love you just because you were good at baseball!" I was incredulous, "He loved you for who you were. He was very proud of you because you were good at baseball because he loved the game but that isn't why he loved you."

"I know that now, Mom."

When Eric was younger, my husband did try to do things with our kids. He coached the boys' baseball teams, played games with them, and helped them with their sports skills. It just seemed that Eric needed something more.

Perhaps, Eric felt my husband preferred working long hours over spending time with him. I'm not sure.

When Eric was home at one point between rehab stints, I told my husband Eric needed him more. He immediately went upstairs to speak to Eric, who was in his room.

"Your mother says that you need me more. What do you need me to do?"

A few minutes later, he came downstairs.

"Eric just told me everything was fine," he said.

In retrospect, I'm not sure if Eric knew or could express in what way he needed his father. If he could have communicated what he thought back then, maybe he wouldn't have felt the way he did.

Deep down inside, Eric knew his father loved him and he loved his father.

He often kissed his father and said, "I love you, Pop."

I grew up with a father, who worked six days a week, and didn't get home until seven o'clock, most evenings. I never felt that he didn't love me or that I needed him more because he worked long hours. He was there. He was the head of our family and we had my mother, who ran the household and was with us each day.

It didn't bother me at all to have a father, somewhat, in the background but it bothered Eric. I wish I could have made Eric feel better about this but I could not.

Suddenly, Eric changed the subject.

"Mom, I can overcome any difficulty that I might face in life because Jesus is my Lord and Savior," he said, his voice calm and confident.

I was touched at how easily he stated his trust and faith.

When Bruce and I went to dinner that evening, Eric and Matthew hung out at the house and played video games.

Sunday morning Eric, his father, and I went out to breakfast. At breakfast, Eric ate a poached egg with a piece of dry whole-wheat toast and fruit. Since June, he'd become health conscious.

He hung around the house and only went outside for an occasional cigarette.

"I'm trying to quit, Mom," he said, "But it's difficult. Everyone I work with, smokes. It's a social thing."

I suggested that he try cutting back to three or four cigarettes a day at work, thinking it might be too much for him to give up smoking completely. Sobriety first.

Eric took a nap that afternoon and left around five o'clock to get to his AA home group meeting on time.

We talked about the following weekend. He said he still planned on coming home. We decided we'd all see Denzel Washington's new movie, *Safe House*. Jessica planned to meet us at the theater and then we'd all go to dinner, as a family. I was already thinking about what I could make Eric to eat, wanting to encourage his healthy eating habits. The better he treated his body, I figured, the less likely he would want to put poison in it. Since June, he'd treated his body like a temple.

I was so happy. All three of my children were healthy. I couldn't have wanted anything more.

32. Shock
February 17, 2012

On my way home from work, I stopped for groceries for Eric's weekend visit. I liked having his favorite foods on hand and also wanted to prepare dishes he could take back to his apartment.

I knelt on the floor, surrounded by bags of groceries, and unloaded them. The phone rang.

I stood up and picked up the kitchen phone. It was Eric's boss.

"Has anyone from the New Haven Police Department contacted you?" he asked.

I panicked.

"No, why? What's wrong?"

"I don't know if it's my place to tell you but I'm sorry to say Eric passed away this morning."

"What do you mean? He died? That can't be! What happened?!"

"His roommates found him this morning in his room. I don't have a lot of details but I was told there was drug paraphernalia near him."

"That can't be. He was home four days ago and he was fine. There's no way he would do drugs. That can't be."

"Eric left work early yesterday to see a doctor because he had a severe earache," he said, "Maybe that had something to do with his death."

I continued asking questions, then abruptly ended the call.

"I can't talk to you anymore," I said. I hung up.

I can't believe this! The nightmare I've played in my mind so often the past few years has come true. No, this can't be. This has to be a mistake. My son, my beautiful boy, cannot be dead. We beat the drugs. We beat the addiction. No, this cannot be true.

I walked into the family room and stood against the wall, sobbing uncontrollably. I was home alone and didn't know what to do. I didn't want to call Matthew, Jessica, or my husband and tell them something so horrible over the phone because, then, they'd have to drive home.

I called a neighbor. When she picked up, I asked, through tears, "Can you come over? I can't be alone right now."

"Is everything okay?"

I was unable to answer her through sobs.

"I'll be right over."

Still crying, I went back to the kitchen to put away the last few groceries. My neighbor flew through the kitchen door and stood by the table, looking at me, puzzled.

I got up from the floor and walked to her, allowing her to hug me.

"The drugs won. Eric died," I cried, "The drugs won."

She calmed me down and we sat in the dining room, both of us in a state of disbelief. Questions and confusion raced through my mind. *How could this be? It doesn't make sense. Eric was doing so well. He was so proud of himself and his sobriety. We were all proud of what he had accomplished over the past eleven months. We had plans. He had a future. No way. This can't be. He can't be dead, and he certainly didn't die from drugs. They must be mistaken. I can't believe it!*

My neighbor called New Haven police for more information but the officer who'd responded to the call wasn't there. No one else could tell us anything, other than what was written in the report.

I just sat, tears in my eyes.

Twenty minutes later, Matthew came home. We told him. He stood in the doorway between the kitchen and dining room, dumbfounded.

"It can't be true," he said, "He was fine just four days ago."

I told him Eric has left work early because of severe ear pain. That was very unlike Eric. He'd work through horrible colds and fevers. He wouldn't leave work to see a doctor, unless something was terribly wrong. He must have been in a lot of pain. It couldn't have been an ordinary ear infection.

We both decided something else must have killed him, a brain aneurysm; perhaps, because there was no way he'd take drugs.

Maybe the police are looking at the wrong report.

Something had to be wrong. I decided I wouldn't believe it, until I saw the autopsy report. I refused to believe what they told me.

33. The Candle
February 2012

We waited until the next day to tell family and friends because I just couldn't get the words out. We were spared the torture, though.

Around ten o'clock as Matthew and I talked about how to break the news to the family, I suddenly said, "Facebook!"

We checked Eric's page. People knew. The messages already piled up on his wall, 'RIP,' 'We will miss you.' We called one of his friends in New Haven and asked her to take down the posts because we hadn't told the family yet.

Some came down but it was already too late. Most of Eric's friends knew he had died by eleven o'clock that night.

Still hoping I'd get to the family first, I rose early Saturday to call my sister in Rhode Island at 8:45. I knew my mother and another sister were scheduled to visit her.

At 8:43 my phone rang. It was my sister in New England.

"Laura just called, hysterical crying," she said, "She told me people had posted things about Eric on Facebook. Is everything okay?"

"No," I said, choking up. "Eric died yesterday."

My mother and other sister had decided not to visit Rhode Island, after all. They were still in New Jersey. I didn't want to tell my mother her grandson had died, over the phone.

I didn't feel like driving anywhere and I didn't feel like calling anyone. So, another of my sisters in New Jersey went to my mother's house to deliver the news.

It wasn't even nine o'clock in the morning and I already was overwhelmed.

My husband was much stronger and drove to his mother's place to tell her in person.

My neighbor, who'd come over when I got the news, called other neighbors to let them know. But she told me, most of them already knew.

The phone rang constantly. People came over. Most brought food, expressed their horror at Eric's death, and stayed a few minutes. They hugged me. They cried with me. They couldn't believe it, either.

We talked about the sadness with those who stayed but we also talked about the past and, surprisingly, laughed at the adventures of Eric and their own children, when they were younger. It was hard to believe I could laugh but the stories comforted me. I was very grateful for their company.

Our families also came over and stayed a few hours. The outpouring of support was overwhelming.

The next few days were filled with activity. I went through them in a daze. We planned the wake and funeral, purchased cemetery plots, and organized the repast. We picked out prayers.

I went shopping for something to wear. I asked Jessica and Matthew to buy clothes to bury their brother in, since all of his were in New Haven.

"We need to bury Eric in a way that would make him happy," Jessica said, crying.

"Buy him clothes you think he'd like," I said.

They went to his favorite clothing store and bought him his favorite sneakers. What a horrible thing for them to have to do.

Eric's friends visited, too. Like everyone else, they were devastated and horrified.

"Even though he always presented himself as a very happy-go-lucky person," I told them, "He had a lot of internal pain and he only showed his pain to me."

One of his friends requested to speak at his funeral. I granted permission as long as he didn't talk about how they used to party.

Jessica and I also decided to speak. My resolve to do this shocked me but I felt I had to. A lot of people knew Eric had problems and struggled with life. I wanted them to know how well he had been doing. I had to tell them he left this earth on top and that my son, my beautiful boy, had been winning against the demons he'd battled for so long.

I wrote a short speech and practiced it over and over.

Approximately one thousand people attended Eric's wake; a number that boggled my mind. Some waited more than an hour to get into the funeral home to pay their respects.

The church was packed for the funeral, too. Many people said they took the day off to attend. A woman, who worked at the church, came in on her day off to serve at the mass. I'd known her many years.

"I want to do it for Eric and your family," she said.

In life, Eric was never convinced he was loved. I hoped that, as he looked down from above, he finally knew how many lives he had touched and how loved he truly was.

Many people shared stories about my son and the positive impact he'd had on them. "He'd always made them laugh," they said.

Many people came down from New Haven, making two trips, one for the wake, another for the funeral. Many of Eric's friends in recovery said they wouldn't have achieved sobriety without him. They told me they loved his smile and his laughter. One asked to put his one-year AA medallion in Eric's casket.

Sleep didn't come easily during this time and immediately after the funeral. When I closed my eyes, I saw Eric screaming and crying. I was horrified at the thought my son was so upset. This vision came to me for a couple of nights.

Then, when I closed my eyes, I had another more peaceful vision. Eric and another figure, their backs to me, walked down a path together. On either side, the path was a cloud-like white. The two of them talked. Sometimes, they sat on a park bench, their backs still to me, and kept talking. Sometimes, they walked into a beautiful wooded area.

Regardless of where they were or what they were doing, they just talked. Eric seemed at ease and happy with this figure. Sometimes, I saw the side of Eric's face. He was always smiling and laughing.

After a couple of nights, I realized the figure was there to calm Eric. I believe Eric was upset that he had died. I believed he was as shocked, as everyone else.

I also determined that the figure was my father in his younger years. I'd often said that Eric needed my father, when he was alive because my husband was always busy working, so we could enjoy a comfortable life. If my father had been alive, he would have filled some of the holes Eric felt from his dad's absence. They seemed to have finally met and, as I'd thought, got along very well.

After many nights, the vision changed again.

Eric carried either a baseball and a glove or a basketball. My father loved sports, especially baseball. As time moved on, they had a catch and shot hoops. Eric was enjoying my father's company, along with that of all the other people I've known who passed away. These visions put me at ease. It seemed my son was okay.

After the funeral, my sister and niece from Rhode Island stayed for a couple of days. My neighbors continued to be great. They called me to take walks or talk and they stopped over to see if I was okay. A couple told me to watch for signs from Eric telling me he was fine.

Truth is, that had already happened.

In the days leading up to the funeral, I occasionally saw the battery-powered candle on my kitchen counter, lit. At first, I was too overwhelmed to pay much attention. Right after the funeral, it was lit again. I asked everyone in the house if they'd turned it on during the past few days. Everyone said no.

I was convinced Eric lit it to tell me he was alright.

34. A Rainbow
March 2012

When I told my principal about Eric's death, I said I didn't know when I'd return to work. I was a teacher, and I worked with a lot of wonderful students as well as kids who, like Eric, found life difficult. How was I supposed to work with those who struggled with the same issues my son had faced?

On my first weekday home after the funeral, I wrote thank you notes. After working on this horrible project for three hours, crying the whole time, I decided staying home was not good for me. That evening, I called my principal and told him I'd return to work the following week.

"It won't be a tearless reentry," I said, "The students will see me cry."

"That will be okay," he replied, "Everyone knows how difficult this will be for you, including the students, and everyone will help you get through it."

The rest of the week, after the funeral, was just as miserable.

I went to the local branch of the bank Eric used, showed his death certificate, and asked to withdraw the money in his savings and checking accounts. The teller took an hour to sort things out. In the end, she told me I had to go to surrogate court because Eric didn't have a will. *Of course, he didn't have a will. He was only twenty-two!*

My cousin accompanied me to court the first time and my sister, the second time. I needed them. I didn't know how to speak to people about what had happened. I couldn't imagine ever speaking about Eric again, without crying. As if burying my son wasn't horrible enough, I had to go through all this legal nonsense to get the few thousand dollars he had.

I took care of other miserable business as well, including returning Eric's prized Christmas present; the pots we'd given him. He never used them because his new apartment already had a stocked kitchen. He loved them, though, and told me to save them, so he'd have them when he moved out on his own. Returning the pots was extremely painful; though, it would have been just as painful to keep and use them.

The store clerk slowly inspected each one to make sure they hadn't been used. She never asked why I brought them back. If she had, I couldn't have answered without becoming hysterical.

On the first day I returned to work, I left my car determined not to burst into tears as soon as I walked into the building. I succeeded.

Twenty feet into the building, I encountered a student.

"Hey, Mrs. Burns, it's great to see you back!" He said.

That's all it took. I walked into my room, tears streaming down my face, and then into the office. I calmed myself before first period. I'd wanted to talk to my students about what happened. I felt something so tragic couldn't be swept under the rug.

But I couldn't address the class. When I started to speak, I cried. At that moment, the principal walked into the room.

"Mrs. Burns has had an extremely rough two weeks," he told them, "It's going to take some time for her to feel better so you need to be extra kind to her."

While he spoke, I composed myself. When he left, we began class.

The rest of the day went smoothly but, toward the end, I realized many students were very uncomfortable seeing me. Some walked into my room with fear written all over their faces. By the end of the day, I realized my returning to work was as difficult for them as it was for me.

Even so, many of my students came in and hugged me. They were wonderful. So were all my colleagues.

My neighbors kept cooking dinners for us, which filled me with gratitude. By Wednesday, I was exhausted. Once home, I lost all energy and just plopped on the couch.

Getting up at five in the morning also was a challenge. I lay in bed feeling paralyzed. Somehow, I forced myself up and moved. I don't know how.

I also avoided people. I grocery shopped only for large orders, going at eight o'clock in the morning on Saturdays. I realized that meeting people I knew would make me cry, and sometimes, I didn't want to feel so sad. If I saw someone I knew in the store, I quickly turned down the nearest aisle, even if I didn't need anything there.

That was my norm for a long time after Eric's death. Sometimes, even a look of sorrow caused my tears to flow.

Going to church also became an ordeal. I didn't speak to God for two weeks. When I did, I began my prayers with, "I'm not happy with you right now, even though I'm still talking to you."

I asked him to take care of Eric.

"Help him find in death, Lord, the peace he couldn't find on earth," I said.

I even attended church, once I decided to do so, in avoidance mode. I went at seven-thirty in the morning, normally too early for me or Monday evening. Occasionally, I saw someone I knew and kept my tears to a minimum. During mass, though, they flowed freely.

I always liked the hour of peace, quiet, and prayer I found in church on Sunday mornings. I reflected on whatever was happening in my life; the good and the bad. I centered myself and gathered the strength to go on.

During the most trying times with Eric, I found church a place of solace. After he died, it was a place of sadness. The quiet, I once found appealing, now reminded me of the sadness that had entered my life. I thought of my son and how he was no longer with me.

I also left work upset. Though I kept it together while working, I cried the second I walked out the building.

At the one-month anniversary of Eric's death, I drove home crying. I'd loaded my car with all the dishes that had come to my house filled with food and dinners that people had prepared. I needed to return them. The day was sunny until I reached my neighborhood, where the weather was unusual. A big black cloud hung over my street. As I rode from house to house, returning dishes, rain fell one minute and the sun beat down the next.

When I got to my house, rain fell in my front yard but not my back yard. Immediately, the phone rang. It was my neighbor.

"Mary, go outside right away," she said, "There's a rainbow in front of your house."

I quickly threw a hoodie over my dress, ran into the rain, and looked up to the sky to see the rainbow.

"You need to come over here to see it," my neighbor's husband shouted from across the street.

I ran across the street and could not believe my eyes. A rainbow arched across my front yard; not high in the sky, as I'd expected. It extended from one side of my property to the other. I saw both ends.

My neighbor and I stood on his front porch, staring in disbelief.

"Do you think Eric has anything to do with this?" I asked.

"That's what I'm thinking," he replied, "I've never seen anything like this."

We remained there, mesmerized, beholding the beautiful rainbow, as it slowly faded.

I felt better than I'd felt all day. I was convinced the rainbow was Eric telling me, once again, that he was okay.

35. Dreaming
August 2012

Six months after Eric died, he came to me in a few dreams.

In the first, he and I talked pleasantly in the family room. I sat on the couch as he sat on a nearby chair.

"What are you doing tomorrow?" I asked him.

He mumbled.

"What are you doing tomorrow?" I asked again.

I could not understand his reply. Finally, I got off the couch and leaned over him.

"I know you don't like it when I ask you the same question over and over again," I said, "But I really can't understand what you're saying. What are you doing tomorrow?"

With that, he looked at me. Chuckling, he lifted the white sheet he used as a blanket over his face and, smiling, turned away from me.

I woke up, heart pounding. The dream was so real. I was convinced I'd really been with Eric. The dream must mean something. After some thought, I decided Eric couldn't answer my question because he's in Heaven, where there are no tomorrows. A sense of peace filled me.

A couple of nights later, Eric came to me in another dream. We hugged each other and sobbed as he said, over and over, "Mommy, I'm sorry. I'm so sorry. I should have called someone. I'm so sorry."

Both of us cried so hard, we fell to the ground, still clinging to one another. As we kneeled, still in an embrace, Eric melted away. I woke up whimpering, my arms across my chest as if I was hugging myself or someone else.

I believe Eric is at peace in heaven but I also think he, sometimes, feels my pain there because we were so close.

"I'll try to cry less," I told him. I didn't want him upset in heaven. I wanted him to have serenity. Eric was tormented during his life on Earth and I didn't want that for him anymore.

"I'm okay," I said, "I'll make it through this. It's okay for me to cry now because I'm only human. If the tables had been turned and I had died, you'd cry for me and find letting go very difficult and painful."

I invited him to visit me again in a dream and smile.

"I love you," I said.

When I closed my eyes, I saw him again. He had wings.

A couple of weeks later, I had a third dream. Eric was older and driving. I was in the front passenger seat.

"Sometimes I drink alcohol, Mom," he said, "I do it to get it out of my system."

Instantly, I worried.

"How often? Once every two weeks? Once a week?"

"No, I have a drink every day."

I panicked but, before I could reply, the car swerved left, landing us in the middle of the road. A group of people, all dressed as if they were running a marathon, came toward us.

"You are in the middle of the road!" I yelled at Eric, "You need to go to the right."

Eric fell asleep at the wheel. The car straightened as it rolled down the road, running over each runner, and causing each to fall backward onto the ground.

Heart pounding, I woke up.

It took some time to calm down. I needed to determine the meaning of that dream, too. *What is Eric trying to tell me?*

In the beginning of the dream, Eric appeared older, as if he hadn't died young. His admission that he drank daily told me that, had he lived, he probably would have struggled with addiction throughout his extended life.

The fact that he fell asleep at the wheel signified his death at twenty-two and the people running toward the car represented all the earthly troubles or demons that would have tormented him, if he'd lived. The people were dressed for a marathon, which I interpreted to mean they were in it for the long haul.

After Eric fell asleep, the car continued to run over and destroy everything that would have troubled him if he'd lived. The dream told me that, in death, Eric destroyed and, therefore, conquered his tormentors. Nothing and no one could cause him any more pain.

36. Woman at the Window
August 2012

Two weeks later, I had a fourth dream. I was in a large, rustic house in a wooded area near a lake. I walked into a back room with large windows, overlooking the lake; passing an old woman, who sat at a table near the windows. She knitted or crocheted. As I walked by, she kept her head down.

I kept going until I looked down and saw I was at the top of a staircase. I hesitated before walking down the stairs and peered into a small, square room to my right. It didn't have a door. The window-sized openings in the room, covered with a strong wire screen, faced the interior of the house. In the room, were two young unkempt children, who I believed were girls. They had black eyes and appeared to have been beaten.

They came to the screen.

"Help us," they said, "Help us."

I looked at the woman by the window. She looked up at me.

"Look at what they did to me," she said, pointing to a black eye.

The woman spooked me. Suddenly, two different children ran into the room. I grabbed both, picked them up, and ran down the stairs, holding them in my arms.

The woman got up from her seat and chased the three of us.

Once outside, I put the two children down. We all ran to the front yard of the house, with the woman in hot pursuit. One of the children ran ahead of me. The other, slower, was behind me. The woman caught the girl, who lagged behind. The child screamed. She did not want to go with the woman.

I whipped around, saw the screaming child, and wondered what to do.

At that point, I woke up, heart pounding.

The dream replayed the next night. It was so vivid that I had to figure out its meaning, too. Although Eric was not in these dreams, I believe they were related to addiction. For me, the old woman represented addiction itself and the children were her victims.

The woman had a black eye because the children fought to get away from her. They sat in the room, beaten physically, mentally, and emotionally. Though they asked me for help, they appeared lethargic and exhausted.

The lack of a door represented the difficulty of escaping addiction. If it were easy, there'd have been a door and the children could have walked through it.

The children, I grabbed and carried down the stairs symbolized the future victims of addiction. I tried to take them away from the woman but was unable to save both. The woman caught the slower one and when I spun around, I asked myself, *Do I save this child or run away from Addiction?*

The dream told me I must do something with Eric's story or, as he would call it, his struggle. I had to do something with the pain that came with living through such a horrific experience with my son.

The dream told me I had a choice to make – fight addiction by helping others or leave this experience behind me and, hopefully, never have to deal with addiction again.

37. A Tree Is Planted
Fall 2012–Winter 2013

Just over eight months after Eric's passing, we headed to New Haven for the first time, since he died. I wanted the city to be a source of healing and happy memories for me. Eric had recovered there, after all, and we'd been happy together on my visits.

But as we drove, I wasn't sure how I'd react to being where my son had died.

That day in Quinnipiac River Park, across the street from where Eric had lived for a few months, friends were planting a tree in his memory. It's a small park; just a narrow, grassy strip of land that runs along the western border of the Quinnipiac River in New Haven's Fair Haven district. The Grand Avenue Bridge, an old swing bridge built in 1900, is visible in the distance.

On either side of the river are buildings that give the area a quintessential New England feel. Across the river, a single church spire peaks through the treetops.

I told everyone, who knew Eric, about the planting and didn't know how many would show for the short ceremony. I also told everyone to bring a picnic lunch so that, after the planting, we could spend time together.

We arrived around noon. A crowd had already gathered where the tree was to be planted. The sky was a beautiful blue with very few clouds. I stepped out of the car, feeling the fall crispness in the air. I wore black jeans, a long-sleeved, dark green shirt, and black jacket. It didn't seem right to wear bright colors, when I still felt so sad.

I hesitated before crossing the street; taking in the scene. Suddenly, I wasn't so sure I wanted to be there. Sadness fell over me. I was in New Haven, the place that had given me so much happiness, the place I had watched my son grow into the young man I knew he could become. But that was no longer the case. It was now a place of grief that always would remind me of the heartache I'd carry the rest of my days.

We would plant a tree in memory of my son. *In memory*. I still had a difficult time using that word. Yet, that's what Eric was in my new world.

I crossed the street and slowly made my way toward the crowd.

My family from New Jersey and Rhode Island greeted me. They each hugged me but I could hardly respond. I felt numb and just stood, staring at the flurry of activity.

At 12:45 p.m., we gathered around the tree in a circle. My niece, Maria, said a few words and then invited others to say something. Many people spoke.

Some talked about how much they missed Eric.

Others talked about how they couldn't have stayed sober without him.

Everyone spoke with love and warmth.

People asked if I wanted to say anything. I couldn't. If I tried to speak, my voice would betray me, the pain in my heart would overwhelm me, and I would cry.

After the ceremony, each person placed a shovelful of soil over the roots of the tree. Everyone helped cover the roots; Eric's friends, my family, and even my eighty-six-year-old mother. I didn't want to help. Why would I want to help plant a tree in *memory* of my son?

The pain behind the reason I was there became sharper. I dabbed my eyes with a tissue and stood, frozen in place, watching.

Once the tree was planted, we ate lunch.

One of Eric's friends organized the event and his old boss paid for platters of sandwiches and cold salads that lined a couple of tables set up near the tree. As people ate, I worked my way through the crowd and thanked everyone for coming.

I also used the time to get some answers. Where did Eric get the drugs that killed him? Maybe he found them in his room and, because he was in so much pain with his ear that evening, decided to use them.

I asked his roommates whether the person who lived in the room previously could have left some drugs behind. Eric had moved into the room of the kid he didn't think was serious about his sobriety. It might have seemed like an absurd question to a recovering addict but, as a mother, searching for answers to her son's untimely death, I needed an answer. They told me the person in that room before Eric had a different drug preference.

I was introduced to a young woman, who knew Eric.

"Two weeks before he died, we were both struggling," she said, "We talked for long periods of time about how hard it had become to stay sober."

I was grateful for her candor but what she said upset me. *How could Eric have been struggling so much when he sounded so positive in the weeks leading up to his death? And if he was struggling, why didn't he pick up the phone and call someone for advice and encouragement?*

It was difficult to understand how someone, who had become such a leader and help to so many others, could not reach out for help. *Was being seen as a leader detrimental to Eric? Did he feel he couldn't admit to weakness because others looked up to him?*

The cool air chilled me and I drew my jacket tighter, remembering the last time I saw Eric less than a week before he died. If he'd been struggling, why, oh why, hadn't he said something?

Maybe, I thought, *just maybe God knew he was going to take Eric and told him, "Go home and say goodbye to your mother."*

After lunch, we waited for the plaque to arrive. It was simple: Eric's name, dates of birth and death, and two words, Beautiful Boy. Passersby would not understand the meaning of those two words but they meant a lot to Eric and me.

After I wrote the poem, we called *Beautiful Boy;* Eric often asked me in his silly voice, "I'm your beautiful boy, Mommy, right?"

I still answer that question in my heart. *Yes, Eric, even though we had many ups and downs during your life, you will forever be my beautiful boy.*

A few weeks after the ceremony, an unsettling thought struck me, as I drove home from work. Two weeks before Eric died, a bolt of electricity had traveled through my body with the thought, *this is when the trap door usually opens.*

I'd dismissed it.

Not this time, I told myself.

It amazed me that Eric and I may have been so connected that I felt his weakness more than one hundred miles away.

In the weeks after that electrical feeling swept through my body, I was more concerned about him than usual. I can't explain why.

When he was home, the weekend before his death, I almost said to him, "You're not thinking of doing something stupid, are you?" and, "If you do drugs now, they'll probably kill you because your body is so pure." My gut was telling me something. Yet, I didn't say a word because the young man before me seemed full of life, mature, and confident. Best of all, he was talking about the future.

I wished I'd said something, though, I can't be sure it would have made a difference

When spring arrived, I remembered all the things we'd planned to do; visit a culinary school in New York City, hike a few places near New Haven, and go to a restaurant to celebrate his one year of sobriety. They were little things but I'd been looking forward to them.

I had nothing to look forward to with Eric any longer. I only had memories.

As the months passed, I realized how much I missed my biweekly visits to New Haven. I loved trying different restaurants with Eric and taking long walks with him. I missed our conversations. I missed seeing his friends. I was just beginning to know them.

Each morning when I woke up, I thought of Eric and he usually was my last thought before I fell asleep, each night. Every day I told him I loved him and that I was sorry for not being able to take away his pain.

I asked the Lord to give him a hug and kiss for me and then I asked that he not let Eric forget me. I certainly would never forget him.

I still questioned many things, though. Why was my son put on this Earth to be tormented the way he was? Why did his life have to be so difficult?

And, why didn't the Lord stop him from taking that fatal dose? I'd prayed over the years, asking the Lord to shine his light before Eric and show him the way. I'd even given him permission to slap him for me, if the thought of doing drugs ever entered his mind again. Why didn't Jesus slap him?

Months after the tree planting, I asked Eric's friends how the young woman I'd met was doing. None of them knew who she was. I thought that odd. Why didn't anyone know her? Sometimes, I think she was the devil in disguise sent to Earth to tempt Eric. The thought of her befriending him gave me an uneasy feeling.

In Eric's final days, I was finally seeing his future.

I was going to throw him a big surprise party, when he graduated culinary school.

He was going to own his own business.

He was going to get married and have two little boys.

He was going to live to be an old man.

And he was going to take care of me, when I got older because I had stood by him during these very difficult years.

What happened? Why did we lose such a hard-fought battle? Why?

I saw a therapist to talk about what had happened and heal. My husband was unable to talk about it. Jessica got too emotional. Matthew was willing to listen but I didn't want to burden him with my sadness.

I unburdened to friends and family as well. Although I tried talking about topics other than Eric and my sadness, the two had a way of entering into many conversations. When you lose someone close to you, especially a child, it's difficult not to talk about them. Not because you want to relive the sadness but because they were such a big part of your life.

I, often, equate Eric's absence to background music. He's always on my mind and in my heart. I feel his presence every day, all day long. But, sometimes, the thought of him comes up front and center and I can't help but to focus on his life, my loss, and the pain.

I probably will never accept what has happened. My life path gave me a son to love and required me to watch helplessly, as he struggled with disease and addiction. I wasn't able to save him from his demons.

But, then, I remember all that's happened since his death; the candle that lights on its own, the dreams, the visions of him smiling and, of course, that amazing rainbow. And I find myself thinking that although *I* couldn't save Eric, maybe he was saved, after all.

Epilogue
Fighting the Old Lady

I have chosen to fight the old lady in my dream.

Most of the years, since Eric died, I've shared my story at an annual student assembly for the eighth-graders that I teach. It's difficult but I feel strongly that they *must* understand that their life choices matter.

Drug education in health classes gives them facts; statistics on addiction, the different drugs that pose a danger. But information from a textbook, though important, can't produce the same emotional impact as a story such as mine.

I show up in the cafeteria after lunch, without warning, and talk to more than one hundred of them. They sit quietly. They listen. Some sob.

I tell them how talented Eric was. I tell them how much pain he was in.

"The drugs took away that pain," I say, "Until the addiction took hold."

I tell them how difficult it was for Eric to leave drugs behind.

I tell them how painful it is for me to go on without him.

"I lost all the things I would have experienced with Eric, if he'd lived," I tell them, "I lost a possible future wedding, a future daughter-in-law, and grandchildren and all the events that go along with having a son and his family in your life; birthday parties, baptisms. The list goes on."

"My son was well and excited about his future and then in an instant, all that was lost due to drugs. My life and the life of my family will never be the same. There will always be a huge hole in my heart and in the hearts of everyone, who loved Eric."

By the time I finish, many students are crying.

I have two hopes; that our story will make them think twice when faced with temptation and that those who are troubled or feel low self-esteem or even self-hatred, recognize themselves and let people help them.

Eric and I talked about speaking at schools together.

"Mom," he said, "If I can get just one kid to think twice about drugs and not go through what I did, speaking at a school will have been worth it."

Each time I speak, I take that thought with me.

I have also shared our story at community programs run by The Center for Prevention and Counseling (TCPC), a nonprofit organization in my county.

I've become involved in an advocacy group organized by the New Jersey chapter of the National Council on Alcoholism and Drug Dependency. It runs programs that help recovering addicts maintain long-term recovery.

I've also taken my message to my state senator and addressed the New Jersey Senate Budget Appropriations Committee on the need for a new treatment protocol for addiction.

Along with another mother, who lost a son to addiction, I spearheaded a fundraising walk hosted by TCPC. The first year, two hundred and twenty-five people attended 'Changing the Face of Addiction,' raising $16,000 to help addicts, without insurance, who need services. By the fourth year, more than five hundred walkers raised more than $57,000.

We both feel we've hit a nerve. TCPC, now, runs the fundraiser and local businesses sponsor it. Groups of people walk, strong and unashamed, in solidarity and in memory of their loved ones. We want people to know long-term recovery is possible and that people, who struggle with addiction, can move forward and take their lives back.

Addiction will always claim lives but, in memory of my son, I resolve to eliminate the stigma around addiction and change the treatment protocol, so people can get the help they need.

Afterword

Before Eric died, we talked about writing this book together. He even read my first version. One of his friends told me he'd begun to write his part. I never found it.

I went ahead with this project to share his struggle, as he'd wanted but, also, because I want readers to walk away with a better understanding of addiction.

First and foremost, no one chooses addiction, a condition that culminates over time and lasts forever. People choose whether to take that first drink or drug but their addiction is not a choice. Many of us can drink socially. Some individuals may even use drugs recreationally. Only after many months, at the Connecticut rehab, did Eric understand why he had become addicted to drugs; they soothed his internal pain, until the addiction took hold.

Since his death, I've spoken to many people in recovery and learned internal pain is a common thread in their stories. A person often continues to use drugs or alcohol to relieve this pain, so they can feel good about themselves. The substances change their brains, causing them to become addicted.

Second, addiction is forever.

My son's demons of self-hatred and low self-worth were always present, even in long-term recovery. I thought Eric had beaten them into submission. I thought we'd won the war. Instead, the demons had been patiently walking alongside him, waiting for an opportunity to enter his psyche again and destroy him.

I also emphasize how difficult it is, even for a family with resources such as mine, to get proper treatment for an individual trying to recover from addiction. A person struggling with addiction, especially a young one needs six to nine-month inpatient treatment, early in their quest to get well.

I've detailed Eric's outpatient and inpatient experiences in these pages. It's clear to me that in the two months between his outpatient treatment, required by our insurance company, and his first thirty-day inpatient rehab program, the drugs tightened their hold on his brain.

After the first rehab, he was sent home without support, when we were told his chances of sustained success were a mere ten percent.

In the three months before Eric's second four-week inpatient rehab program, the drugs tightened their hold on his brain yet again. Yet, in the course of that second rehab, our insurance company wanted to cut treatment after two weeks. If Eric had had cancer, there would have been no question as to whether he got proper treatment.

The medical community clearly considers addiction an illness. The National Institute on Drug Abuse describes addiction as 'a chronic disease characterized by drug seeking and use that is compulsive or difficult to control, despite harmful consequences.' It seems to me that insurance companies don't see it that way.

Failing at staying sober because of this revolving door of treatment only added to Eric's feelings of low self-worth. It only made it more difficult for him to think he'd ever get better. And the feeling of being a failure or not being worthy is often why a person becomes addicted to begin with.

During his speech at the AA meeting in Massachusetts a month before he died, Eric said this about his time at the Texas rehab, "Looking back and knowing what I know now, I actually felt some relief there. It was the only inpatient rehab that I've been to that I was comfortable in."

Yes, he felt relief and comfort there. What if he was able to stay at that rehab for another six to nine months? Would the relief from his pain have continued? Would he have been able to sustain long-term recovery?

I will always wonder if Eric would still be here today if he'd been given long-term treatment, when he first asked for help.

Between the airline tickets, halfway house, medication, insurance copays, therapists, and nine months at the Connecticut rehab, Eric's treatment cost us around thirty-five thousand dollars. While I'm grateful we could foot such an expense, I have to wonder how those, without resources, can help their addicted loved ones.

It seems that, without resources, the only time someone gets treatment is when they get arrested and end up in jail. Then, depending on the state, it's sometimes mandatory.

Perhaps, the much-discussed opiate crisis in this country is partly due to the fact that individuals, who want to recover from addiction, have a difficult time getting proper and timely treatment. We need a new treatment protocol, now.

On another medical note, Eric showed signs of mental illness, when he was only seven years old. Usually, mental illnesses don't become apparent until puberty. Ten years later, as a High School senior, he was diagnosed with Hepatitis B.

I will always wonder if the undetected high levels of the virus in his bloodstream crossed his blood-brain barrier, causing his depression and psychosis. Eric's psychiatrists confirmed a possible connection but his two liver specialists did not.

Why such a disconnect among medical communities? If the psychiatric community is correct and there is a connection, why isn't the pediatric community aware of it? If my pediatrician had been aware, he may have had Eric tested for the virus at age ten, when I first brought my concerns to him.

All children in a high-risk category for the virus, such as my son and daughter born in South Korea, should have routine blood work done at an early age; even if they received the vaccine, as Eric had. That's the only way to ensure they don't have the virus.

Lastly, I want people to understand that, once an addiction takes hold, life becomes a living hell for the addicted person and all who love that individual. It's painful to watch someone you love lose control of their own brain. It's difficult to watch someone make bad decision after bad decision because drugs have hijacked their brain, rendering them incapable of thinking clearly. It's heartbreaking to watch a bright person spend so much time chasing the drugs that their brain demands.

Our culture often portrays individuals, who struggle with addiction, as worthless. They can be viewed as people who don't matter and are not worth saving. I had those thoughts before my experience with Eric but I now know that's not the case.

My son was not worthless. He was troubled. He was a person with abundant talent, which he was unable to see, A beautiful individual, who could not appreciate his beauty. He was my child. He was one of the loves of my life. He was worth saving.

Appendix in Eric's Own Words

The following writings were found in a notebook Eric kept during his stay at the Connecticut rehab. The first couple of pages include some poems he scribbled upon his arrival. The rest are in response to readings required of him during Phase One of the program.

Scared and lonely, alone I sit
Sadness fills this darkened pit.
Will I ever make it out alive?
I fight and scream just to survive.
Clawing to get out of my lifeless body

All alone in a dark room,
A gleam of light shines through.
Can I make it to the light?
Another day filled with struggle;
Weak and empty from the fight.
Just trying to make it through another night.

Saddened mother,
Angry Sister,
Broken son,
Hands blistered.
Moving backwards,
Stomach turning.
Dope sick,
Mind churning.
Crying mother, angry sister.
Broken son, hands blistered.
Dope sick, empty mind.
Moving backwards.
Sitting alone, wondering how did I ever get here

What my future holds is still a mystery and unclear
Thoughts race through my head, of what I could have had
The story of a boy with everything, whose now broken and sad
Feelings rush through his once useful and potential brain
Mistakes from the past still driving him insane

The greatest woman in the world
Couldn't ask for a better mother
Stuck by my side

Dear Mom,

Thank you for everything you've done. I'm trying hard to win this war on drugs and evil.

Trying hard to fight these demons, so home and family, I had to leave them.
To make myself more proud and strong.
For their trust and love, I will always long.
Tears fall every night that I'm away, but in my heart they always stay.
A mother and father I could never have better.

3/24/11

Day 1 – First Full Day

Met with Eddie, who seems like a very chill person, and am looking forward to talking with him more.

Couldn't sleep last night because of Mom and Jessica.

Started crying for about twenty minutes.

Feel like shit but don't want to go home yet.

Looking forward to this new adventure.

Week 1 – Gratitude List

Things to still be grateful for

I feel like I don't deserve anything because of all of the damage I've caused.

My mother,

Through everything she has stuck right by my side and helped me in every single way she could.

The rest of my family

Though it's getting harder, they still love and support me.

Having another chance to get clean

This is something that I'm grateful for because I don't feel that I deserve it but want nothing more than to win this battle.

My health

It feels good to still be healthy and have no real health problems and still be alive, after all of the harm that I've caused my body.

Freedom

Though I don't feel completely 'free,' I am not in jail and I am free from the death grip of drugs for today.

A last chance to make my parents proud.

With all of the love and support they have shown me through my whole life, they deserve to see all of their hard work pay off. They were perfect parents and don't deserve to bury their son.

A chance to build a sober network
I've never really had sober friends and a lot of people here feel this is such a great place and program.

A chance to get my body back into shape
Grateful for this, because gaining weight is a big reason I use.

My mother
I put this again because she is the most important person in my life and I would put her happiness before mine every day of the week.

Week 1 – Doctor's Opinion
The doctor's opinion really sunk in with me because I could really relate with a lot of the things that were discussed in the chapter. I feel there is a ton of truth to what is said and though I know and have heard a lot of what was talked about, it was reassuring and gave me hope to hear there is a way out of this miserable feeling.

My favorite line in the chapter that I could best identify with was, "Although he gives all that is in him, it often is not enough."

I can really relate with that sentence because, at many times, I feel like there was nothing more that I wanted than to stop using and I would sit and try as hard as I could to get busy and not use for that day but I would always end up using by the end of the day.

Hopelessness is another feeling that I can absolutely identify with. As of right now, it is one of the strongest feelings in my body. Over the past two years of my life and everything that has happened, I feel like there is no hope for a person like me and that I am only capable of getting high or die trying. Even though I can see this working around me and see other people rising above this and getting better, I just feel that for myself, personally, there is no hope.

Also, the writer talks about knowing a lot of cases where the alcoholics tried other methods, which failed completely. That hits me hard because I have been in treatment various other times and tried to do everything my way or a way of others and every time I failed miserably. I relate well when the writer says that an alcoholic's brain must be cleared first, so that he can fully understand and accept what the program has to offer. I have never given that chance for my brain to clear because I'm always stuck in my thoughts or racing feelings through my head on where I'll be later in life and things like that. Doing that, all the time, has never given me a fighting chance in this program. It's hurt me very badly and never given me the open-mindedness to fully grasp and work the program.

Another thing that really, really, really set in with me is the line on pg. xxxi, where the writer says, "And deciding his situation hopeless, had hidden in a barn determined to die."

I really relate with this because I have been at this point a few times in my life. The last time being very recent and less than a month ago. While I didn't hide in a barn, I know the feeling of wanting to die and hiding alone and feeling like life is not worth it anymore.

With that all said, I really do like the doctor's opinion and can really relate to it. And while I have heard all of this stuff before and know that the program can work, it was just reassuring to read this chapter.

Week 2 – Experience with Getting Sober

The first time I tried to get clean was in November 2009 and I was 19 years old. I went to an inpatient treatment program in Texas. I knew I needed help but it was hard to admit I was an addict and my heart was only about fifty percent into it, mainly to please my parents.

So, I stayed there for thirty days and came back home. I'd just come out of the fog in my head and thought I was ready to stay clean. But I went home, stopped working a program, remained the same arrogant asshole, and continued to do the next wrong thing. It wasn't long before I got high again because of that, maybe a week.

I ripped and roared for two months and in February 28, 2010, I checked back into inpatient. This time in Florida. After thirty days, I stayed in a halfway house until August 2010 and was basically a dry drunk. Still miserable, just staying clean because of circumstances. I went home in August after having about five and a half months 'clean' and used almost immediately because I was miserable for so long and finally saw a way out.

Over the last seven months, I became my worst and tried to clean up at times, anyway. I thought that would work, nothing worked.

I came to the conclusion I needed long-term help, so I decided to come here. Working with a sponsor has already shown me a light and makes me feel a little better.

Week 2 – Things to Change
   Spiritual malady
   Ego
   Getting out of myself
   Being able to help others
   Anger
   Getting along with others/helping
   Fear

Week 2 – Willingness to Change

My willingness is high to change all the things on that list; plus, just everything about me. Working with my sponsor and doing everything he tells me to do is my first step and it is already helping me out. My ego will be the hardest to change but I feel, also, the most important. Until I change that I feel I will continue to do bad things, make choices, and continue to feel miserable.

Getting out of myself is important because my mind is a dark and awful place right now. When I'm alone in my own thoughts and isolating, I wanted to use the most, so I feel this is really important for me to do.

I know to stay sober I am going to have to help others. I'm very willing to do this because I know it is something that makes me happy. I've never helped another addict or alcoholic but when I'm ready, I feel I would love the chance. This also helps to get me out of myself, so I think that's very important and good.

My anger is a big problem sometimes and it could get me into trouble. I feel that if I cannot change the way I feel, which I don't think I can, I just need to learn to control the way that I react to it and how I harness that aggression and what I focus it on and do with it.

During a long time in my active addiction, I didn't have healthy relationships with anyone and stopped talking to basically everyone I used to know, besides my parents and dealer. So, I feel I need to change that to get sober and stay sober.

Fear is my biggest thing, I feel, that I have to overcome. While I will never admit this to anyone, it is what I am most scared of. Fear of tons of things. I feel the biggest though, is fear of succeeding or maybe fear of failing. I'm not sure which one it is; maybe, both. I'm so worried I won't succeed because all I've done in the past is fail. But I feel like that is because I have never given myself the chance to succeed because I don't feel worthy of it.

All of these things I am absolutely, hundred percent willing to change about me, so I don't have to keep turning to the only solution I know, which is drugs and alcohol.

Week 2 – Step One, 12 and 12

I liked this really a lot and I could relate to a lot of what was talked about in the chapter. It was good to read because it helped me get a better understanding of step one. It opens the chapter saying, "Every natural instinct cries out against the idea of personal powerlessness."

I really relate to that because it was a big hang up for me, for a very long time. For years, I just didn't want to admit that I could be powerless. Then, I relate to the first sentence of the second paragraph that there is no other kind of bankruptcy like alcohol. I really relate to that cause nothing can bring me to my knees like that.

This time I feel completely defeated, so I relate to what they say about that and I'm glad that is what you need to feel in order to start feeling better. I also relate to the humbling himself part because this has been a very humbling experience and, in the past, my ego has hurt me bad. I think that this whole time I've been trying to get clean, step one has been the hardest for me.

Figuring out whether I felt I was an addict or not, took a lot of trying for me. I had to literally and personally feel all of the pain and suffering all for myself and someone telling me about it wasn't good enough. I think that was a very important part in why it took me so many tries to get clean.

Week 3 – Qualities I Like

My ability to make people feel better
The love I have for my family
Kindness and generosity
My understanding of my disease

Week 3 – Actions Taken to Help Others

This will be a short paper because until now all I have cared about is myself. I never in my life have tried to get outside myself and really help others. It's always been me, me, me. I have been helpful to others in a few ways before, though.

Since my mother has always been so supportive, I've taken as many actions as I could in order to help her. I have always gone out of my way to help clean the house and cook while she was at work because she has no other help with that kind of stuff.

Other small actions have just been helping to guide my brother in the right direction because I never want him to go through what I have had to deal with over my lifetime. It's only been a small part but I've tried as hard as I could.

The last thing that I can really think of is that I worked my last job in a group home with adults with developmental disabilities, helping them with everyday living. Thinking back on it, helping my clients, at that job, was probably the most fulfilling thing I've ever done in my life.

Now, I can also say that helping the newcomer here at the rehab. While I am still fairly new at this process, I feel that I have been given a gift and can use that to help others.

Week 3 – What I Miss About Getting High

There are a lot of things that I miss about getting high. I mean obviously the initial first rush of getting high on opiates that I experienced the first time I used but it's also so much more than that, too. I really just miss the whole process of getting high. The driving down to the cop spot, the moments you wait right before the dealer serves you, finally getting that dope in your hand after you woke up sick, opening and smelling the drug, and the process of loading a needle, tying off, and then seeing the blood rush into the needle knowing you just hit a vein, then pushing the plunger down, knowing that complete pleasure and relief of all pain and worries, and just knowing in moments all the fucked-up shit you did to get where you're at won't matter or bug you anymore. That's what I miss the most.

The lifestyle thing. I mean I do miss the fast-paced life of when I partied hard but once I really found opiates, all of that stopped and all I did was hang out alone and sulk in my own sorrow. I was lonely and I wanted to die.

So, all in all, and thinking about the last week and my last run, I really don't miss anything anymore. I am so sick and tired of stealing from and breaking my parents' hearts. I'm tired of family members and girls not wanting anything to do with me. I'm tired of losing jobs I love and having no money. I'm tired of wondering if I'll be okay the next day.

I honestly just want to find the missing piece that has been burdening me my entire life and solve this problem, once and for all.

Week 3 – Remaining Abstinent from Relationships

This one is tough for me because there is a girl in my life I no longer have but feel like I can get again. But just from that feeling, it kind of proves the point and makes me see why I shouldn't be in a relationship.

Just the emotional ups and downs and the basic roller-coaster ride that it can be, is the main reason. I feel like I'm not equipped or ready to deal with those feelings and problems yet, without using to get through it. For example, if I did start to fall for a girl this early in my recovery and then she just broke up with me or cheated on me, I couldn't say with certainty that I wouldn't use over that.

Not only that, but I can't take care of myself right now or, at least, haven't been able to thus far, so taking care of another human is out of the question. I really don't need the drama, aggravation, and headache that come along with it.

They say that the first thing that you put in front of your sobriety is the second thing that you lose. Meaning that first you lose your sobriety, then you lose the thing you put in front of it.

During the first year, I feel the main focus should be solely on recovery and that's why I feel I should remain abstinent from relationships.

Week 4 – Relationship with My Family

My relationship with my family is still very strong, for the most part. Coming into this program, at the end of my last run, some things got bad.

At one point, my sister told me that she didn't want to speak to me anymore and at the time, she was living at home and told me not to even look at her anymore. Thankfully, since I made the decision to come here, the tension has been eased a little bit. We spoke today, 3/31/11, for about ten minutes and everything seemed much better.

My relationship with my brother is very good and he is very understanding and supportive. It feels weird because he is younger than me, so I think that I should be the one giving him advice but, sometimes, it's the other way around. I've tried to guide him in some ways and I really stay on him to make sure he doesn't make any decisions that will lead him down the paths that I went down.

All in all, my sister and brother and I have a very close relationship because that was just the way that we were raised. When we were young, we did a lot of things together and they always try to still do things with me. I haven't been there when I should have been, though, and it's something I really want to work on.

My father…is as supportive and loving as any other father in the world can be, but in his own ways and the way he feels is right. I'm not saying it isn't right, but, sometimes, just not the way I needed to be loved or feel supported. I think it's mostly my fault but I hold a lot of resentments against him. Now that time has passed, I see it is really just me being selfish. Other than that, we have a solid relationship.

When I was younger, we did a lot together and he came to all of my sports games but that was really all he did and thought that, that was all I needed. Through my recovery, my father has been there for me every step of the way; giving me many chances to overcome this. When I was in treatment in TX and FL, he visited me in both places, which really surprised the hell out of me but, at the same time, made me feel very good about myself.

I saved my mother for last because she is the most important person in my life. There aren't enough good words in the dictionary to describe my mother. She is the sweetest, nicest, most caring, most giving, kind, thoughtful, forgiving, loving, and generous person I have ever met in my life. She is not only my mom but she is my best friend, my number one fan, my support, my trust, and my confidant. I could never ask, want, need, or even, pray or dream for a better mother.

As far as our relationship goes, it's been very good. My mother has been supportive of me and stuck by my side through all the bullshit I've been putting her and everyone else through. I'm not sure why but, even though I've hurt her so many times, she still loves me with all her heart and it's probably what has kept me alive. Because of that, I have tried to stay as close as I could possibly stay with her; even through my active addiction. I love her more than anything in the world and want her to be happy as much as I want me to be happy.

Week 4 – Emotions I Have a Hard Time With
  Fear
  Anger
  Security
  Self-Esteem
  Sadness
  Happiness
  Boredom

Week 4 – Spirituality

Spirituality meant nothing to me until the last few days really. Now, over the past three days, it has come to mean a lot to me.

Spirituality is something that all people have. Some people embrace it easily and some people have to take actions to remove things, which are blocking them from being spiritual. Spirituality is not what you believe in but it is the actions that you take to be better connected with God. It is taking actions to become more aware of what is around you and how you can be better suited to help others.

Week 4 – Spiritual Experience

The reading gave me hope that I will recover but is also exactly what I am going through now. I know that my spiritual outlook must change in order to stay sober. To me, it means that as long as you stay willing, honest, and open minded, spiritual experience will happen; whether quickly or slowly and whether you realize it right away or not.

Week 4 – Letter to Parents

Dear Mom and Dad,

I know my words aren't worth much these days, but I wanted to tell you that I love you and miss you more than anything.

Also, I wanted to thank you for this opportunity to get clean and I promise you I will take full advantage of everything around me. Thank you for all of your support and for being here for me still after all of the things I've put you through.

I want you to know that you did a perfect job raising me and loving and caring for me. You couldn't have done anything better and none of this is your fault.

Again, thank you and I love you.

Love,
Eric

CPSIA information can be obtained
at www.ICGtesting.com
Printed in the USA
LVHW021316040720
659735LV00008B/154